Beyond the Gate:

A Texas Ranch Quilt
in Six (BOM) Applique Blocks

by Margaret Bucklew

My special thanks to my husband, Phillip for his support and encouragement in all of my endeavors. We brainstorm much of the time to come up with just the right patterns, books, websites, illustrations, home building, businesses, and life.

Also thanks to our daughter Mindee. With her sense of humor, she possesses the ability to enhance terminology, inspiration and analysis. Plus, she brings us dinner all the time. :)

Marguerita McManus always shares her editing, quilting, publication, and marketing expertise with the quilting community, of which I am a part. She truly is one willing to go the extra mile to help someone. Many thanks to you, Marguerita.

I would like to thank Katy Pannell, Sarah Cline, and Dawn Hurney for testing this quilt pattern. Their completed quilt photos are available for you to view at http://www.patterns2quilt.com/tt201bg.html. I hope you'll take a moment to see each of their quilts!

Chiseled in Cloth
P.O. Box 112
Poolville, Texas 76487

www.chiseledincloth.com

First Print Edition

ISBN - 978-1-936826-11-7

Table of Contents

introduction

The inspiration for this quilt came from looking out a window onto our prairie ranch land and experiencing nature and all things that evoke a warm fuzzy feeling. You never know what to expect beyond a gate; in our case, windmills, gardens, birds perched on their homes, flowers, ladybugs, butterflies, old wagon wheels, and gates were all quite visible from my second story window. It seemed like the perfect time to share them with you.

The cover page for each of the monthly blocks includes a personal note about the story behind the block; how and why the quilt block spoke to me. I hope it speaks to you as well.

Thinking quilters might enjoy a block of the month a bit shorter time-frame than twelve months, I began the design to be completed within a six month period. Who doesn't want to hurry up and get the quilt on the bed, or give as a gift!

This fusible applique quilt has several monthly blocks that may be used as smaller, individual quilts as well. I refer to them as break out quilts. The wind-mill, the wheelbarrow and flower pots, and the birdhouse would each make fun, wall quilts. Just add a few borders, and you're all set.

This pattern is really for an experienced quilter, not that the entire quilt is challenging, but the wagon wheel in the birdhouse block requires just the right touch in positioning the spokes.

Each month has a cover page with a story about the block, yardage, how to, positioning, and pattern pieces pages. Ample illustrations accompany each of the pages.

Three quilt testers have tested this pattern; however, if you have any issues with it, please email me and I will be happy to help. Please put "beyond the gate quilt pattern" in the subject line, so I'll be certain to spot it. My email is margaretbucklew (at) yahoo (dot) com.

I hope you enjoy putting this together as much as I enjoyed designing it for you. Please send me a photo of your completed quilt!!

Beyond the Gate

Beyond the Gate

Fabric, Supplies & General Directions

Quilt finished size: 92 " x 109"

This is a fusible web applique pattern. Limited applique choices are included

Fabric requirements are for fabric NOT pre-washed

Fabric totals for entire quilt:
(individual months will have fabric totals for that specific month)

Blocks fabric entire quilt:
1 1/2 yd green
1 3/4 yd gold
4 1/2 yd dark purple
1 1/2 yd light purple
9 yd. backing fabric

Applique fabric:
Applique fabric requirements are listed on general directions, page 2

Many of the pieces will only need fat quarters or scraps

Paper backed fusible web:
12 yards for entire quilt

Each month lists individual fusible web requirements

Binding:
450"
3/4 yd for 2 1/2"

Batting:
98" x 115"

Blanket Stitch	
Satin Stitch	
Zig Zag Stitch	

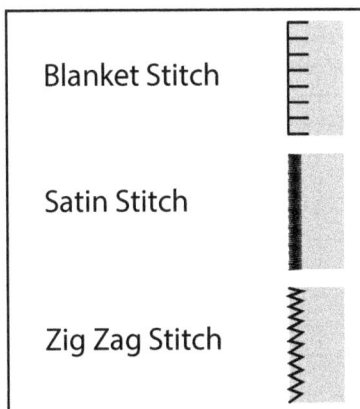

A Few Applique Basics

Fusible web method – paper backed fusible web has a sticky side and a paper side. Trace the design on the paper side. Cut the fusible web larger than the traced image, and press to the wrong side of the fabric. When cooled, cut along the traced lines. Because you will use the traced edge as the final edge, don't cut any extra as a turning allowance.

Remove the paper and following the manufacturer's instructions, press to the wrong side of the fabric. I find it easier to remove the paper if you wait overnight or for a few hours. It seems to harden the sticky part more and causes the paper to curl. If the paper is stubborn, I use a straight pin to score about a 1/8" area from the edge of the paper. Then, just slightly fold outward along the scored line, which allows the edges to protrude, making it easier to clutch the paper.

Use a blanket stitch, satin stitch or zig zag stitch to attach the applique pieces. I use a zig zag stitch width of 1.5 and a length of .8, sometimes adjusting width & length as the size of the pieces change.

Heat and Bond, Steam a Seam, and *WonderUnder* are brands of fusible web. I prefer *WonderUnder* and buy it by the bolt. Many quilters love *Steam a Seam.*

Needleturn method – I love needleturn. It's relaxing and produces a beautiful finish; it makes the edges invisible. As with any hand stitching, it is more time consuming than machine appliqué.

Trace around a template (Mylar or heavy card stock) and cut approximately 1/8" outside the marked area. You will need that scant area to turn under as you work. I use a needle to turn the work slightly ahead of where I will stitch. Using matching thread so it will disappear, take a stitch or two and turn the next area. As you work, continue trying to catch in only the edges of the fabric.

Freezer paper/starch method – I have only used this approach a time or two, but some quilters prefer this technique. My preference is fusible web.

Trace the design onto the shiny side of the freezer paper (larger than the traced area); press that to the dull side of another piece of freezer paper. You will end up with both a shiny and dull side as if you hadn't pressed them together. The double weight helps hold the shape. Then cut out the shape on the drawn lines and press it to the wrong side of the fabric.

To have an edge to turn under, cut the shape out 1/4" away from the freezer paper shape. Spray a little starch into the lid and when the foam settles, use a small brush to brush the wrong side 1/4" seam allowance with starch. Turn the edges toward the freezer paper and press. When it is completely pressed and dried, remove the freezer paper and adhere it to the desired medium using any preferred method.

Reference:

www.youtube.com is an excellent way to learn about appliqué. Type in the search area "how to appliqué". There are thousands of quilters willing share their expertise with you. I'm certain you have experienced how quilters love helping one another, and on YouTube you actually watch them as they work.

www.amazon.com offers detailed information on hand and machine appliqué in book format. Type "how to appliqué" in the search box and you'll find a complete listing of books with numerous tips for working with appliqué.

Beyond the Gate

Fabric Requirements

Quilt finished size: 92" x 109"

Paper backed fusible web:
12 yards for entire quilt

Blocks fabric entire quilt:
1 7/8 yd green
1 3/4 yd gold (if same gold is used for flowers throughout) total=2 3/4 yd
4 1/2 yd dark purple
1 1/2 yd light purple
8-9 yd. backing fabric

***Applique fabric repeated throughout the quilt
totals needed for entire quilt:***

gold .... 1 yd.
orange .... 1/8 yd.
lt. green .... 1/8 yd.
med. green .... 1/8 yd.
red .... 1/8 yd.
black .... 1/8 yd.
green .... 1/2 yd.

Individual listings noted per month

Applique/block fabric by month:

Month1:
flowers (gold) .... ½ yd.
flower centers (orange) .... 3 ½" x 15"
light leaves (lt. green) .... 13" x 9"
medium leaves (med. green) .... 13" x 9"
ladybug body (red) .... 16" x 8"
ladybug head (black) .... 9" x 9"
ladybug spots/antennae (black) .... 9" x 9"
ladybug eyes (orange) .... 4" x 5"
blocks: .... 1 ¼ yd. green, ¾ yd. gold

Month 2:
flower (gold) .... 11" x 9"
flower centers (orange) .... 3" x 3"
light leaves (light green) .... 3" x 9"
medium leaves (med. green) .... 3" x 9"
gloves (med. pink) .... 7" x 10"
wheel & spokes (dk. brown) .... 11" x 12"
wheelbarrow structure [W3-8] (lt. brown) .... ¼ yd.
bucket front (lt. brown) .... 20" x 7"
bucket back (dk. brown) .... 15" x 4"
block: .... 39" x 20½" gold

Month 3:
tulips (yellow, blue, red) .... 7" x 7" ea.
stem/leaves (green) .... 18" x 20"
gate handle (dk. purple) .... 2" x 6"
gate hinges (dk. purple) .... 5" x 10"
nails (dk. purple) .... 5" x 6"
blocks: .... 1 ½ yd. light purple, ½ yd. dark purple

Month 4:
flowers (gold) .... 12" x 9"
flower centers (orange) .... 2" x 2"
light leaves (lt. green) .... 4" x 6"
medium leaves (med. green) .... 4" x 6"
windmill center (dk. brown) .... 8" x 8"
windmill blades (tan) .... 28" x 17"
windmill frame [C6-C10] (med. brown) ...... 52" x 11"
watering can (lt. purple) .... 14" x 9"
watering can 4 square (pink, yellow, grn, blue) .... 3" x 3" ea.
vine (green) .... 29" x 12"
cacti (green) .... 9" x 18"
vane (med. brown) .... 8" x 14"
bird (blue) .... 9" x 8"
bird wing (lt. blue) .... 2" x 4"
block: .... 35 ½" x 66 ½" purple

Month 5:
flowers (3) (gold) .... 17" x 8"
flower centers (3) (orange) .... 4" x 4"
light leaves (lt. green) .... 13" x 8"
medium leaves (med. green) .... 13" x 8"
vines (2) fabric or ¼" fusible bias tape (green)..... 12" x 31"
birdhouse pole (lt. purple) .... 8" x 60"
wagon wheel (tan) .... 16" x 30"
wagon wheel inside/outside (2) (dk. brown) .... 16" x 30"
spokes (red) .... 18" x 26"
watering can (red) .... 15" x 10"
watering can 4 square .... 3" x 3" ea.
bird (blue) .... 9" x 7"
bird wing (lt. blue) .... 24" x 17"
rocks, light (lt. grey) .... 24" x 17"
rocks, shadow (med. grey) .... 16" x 12"
front axel (lt. grey) .... 7" x 6"
rear axel (med. grey) .... 7" x 8"
birdhouse roof [H1 & [H4] (red) .... 10" x 12"
birdhouse front [H3] (gold) .... 12" x 6"
birdhouse frame [H2] (med. brown) ...... 15" x 13"
remaining birdhouse pieces (med. brown)......... 8" x 8"
block: .... 34" x 72 ½" purple

Month 6:
flowers [7] (gold) .... 17" x 4"
flower centers [7] (orange) .... 4" x 3"
light leaves (lt. green) .... 3" x 5"
medium leaves (med. green) .... 3" x 5"
ladybug heads [7] (black) .... 7" x 3"
ladybug body [7] (red) .... 14" x 4"
ladybug eyes [14] (orange) .... 2" x 3"
ladybug antennae [14] (black) .... 5" x 2"
ladybug spots [21] (black) .... 3" x 3"
hat (tan) .... 14" x 9"
hat brim (med. pink) .... 5" x 1"
hat ribbon (med. pink) .... 6" x 4"
flower pots [5] (dk. brown) .... 17" x 7"
tulips [5] (yellow, red, blue) .... 3" x 3" ea.
stem/leaves [5] (green) .... 10" x 8"
blocks: .... ⅝ yd. green, ⅜ yd. gold

My father was a career Air Force man, and yes, I am a proud Air Force Brat. Having spent my youth in places many children would never have the pleasure of visiting, had a profound impact on me as a person.

A time-frame of no more than two or three years in one location was actually quite exciting. Saying goodbye to friends wasn't easy, but meeting new friends was never an issue.

Where else could you play outside and look up to see one after another paratroopers descend from the back of an airplane, feel totally secure with military personnel everywhere, and travel the world?

My father's desire, when he retired, was to "live 40 miles from nowhere". He had spent so many years within military barracks and housing, he wanted to live his retirement in a vast surrounding of open space and beautiful land in his home state of Texas. He didn't live to see it, but I have fulfilled his dream...I live "40 miles from nowhere". Well...almost 40 miles. :)

As I looked out on our land and saw the spaciousness before me, it occurred to me to try to spread his vision of splendor and share it with you through the medium of a quilt.

As you progress through the months working on this quilt, I hope you will experience some of that vision he held so dear.

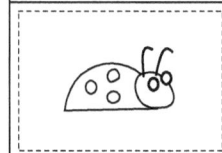

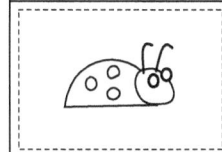

Beyond the Gate

Beyond the Gate

Unit A

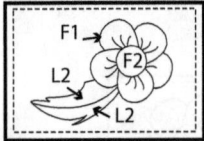

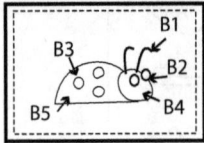

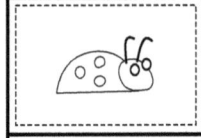

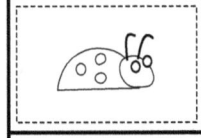

Fabric Requirements:

Blocks:
1 ¼ yd. green
¾ yd. gold

Applique:
flowers ....½ yd.
flower centers ....3 ½" x 15"
light leaves .... 13" x 9"
medium leaves .... 13" x 9"
ladybug body ....16" x 8"
ladybughead.............................9" x 9"
ladybug spots/antennae ....9" x 9"
ladybug eyes.............................4" x 5"

Paper backed web (17"):
1 ⅜ yd.

Stabilizer:
To prevent fabric puckering, use your favorite type of stabilizer behind the appliqué pieces. Tear away stabilizer is a good choice for this purpose.

Thread:
Matching or contrasting thread, as you prefer.

Suggestion:
Use two different colors for the flower petals, one lighter than the other. Embellish the flower with embroidery thread.

For added emphasis, put long running stitches within each of the blocks.

Beyond the Gate

Unit A

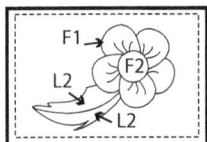

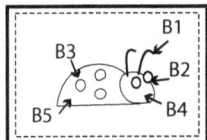

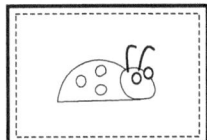

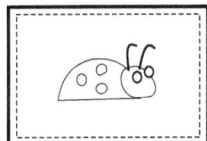

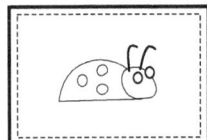

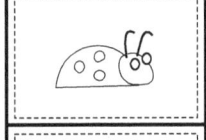

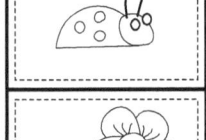

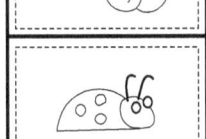

Rotary Cutting
- Green: Cut [2] 18 ½" x width of fabric (wof)
  then, cut [5] rectangles 18 ½" x 12 ½"
- Gold: Cut [2] 12 ½" x (wof)
  then, cut [4] rectangles 18½" x 12 ½"

Green Blocks with flowers
- Trace applique pieces on the paper backed web material
- Press paper backed web to the wrong side of the applique fabric
- Cut out applique pieces

On a teflon or applique sheet:
- **Flower Unit**
  - Create a flower unit by overlapping [5] petals [F1] in a circular shape
  - Place the center circle [F2] over the petals
  - Press
  - Repeat the process for [4] more petals
- **Leaf Unit**
  - Create a leaf unit by overlapping the light [L1]/dark [L2] pieces
  - Press
  - Repeat the process for [4] more leaves

Complete the block
- Alternating positions, place leaf and flower on green background
- Press

Gold Block with ladybugs
Trace applique pieces on the paper backed web material
- Press paper backed web to the wrong side of the applique fabric
- Cut out applique pieces

On a teflon or applique sheet:
- Create a ladybug unit by placing the head [B4]/body [B5]/eyes [B2], antennae [B1], and spots [B3] on the body
- Press
- Repeat the process for [3] more ladybugs

Complete the block
- Place ladybug on gold background
- Press

Applique
- Use a tear away stabilizer behind each block and applique the edges using a blanket stitch, satin stitch, or close zig zag stitch

Create Unit A
- Alternating green/gold blocks stitch all blocks together along the 18 ½" edge to form Unit A
- Unit A size is 18 ½" x 108 ½"

Optional: On the inside of each block use embroidery thread to create long running stitches about .25" from the seam & embroider french knots into the flower centers. Embroider or thread paint shadow lines within each petal.

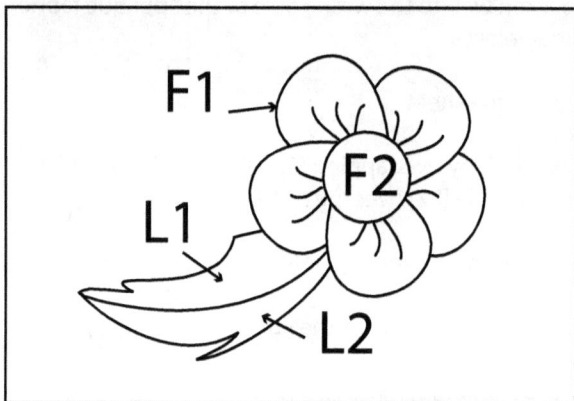

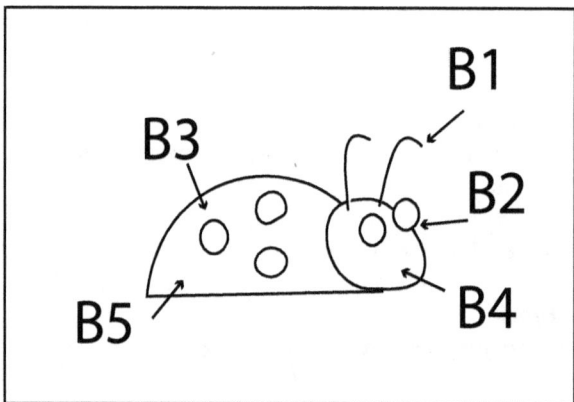

Pattern reversed for tracing

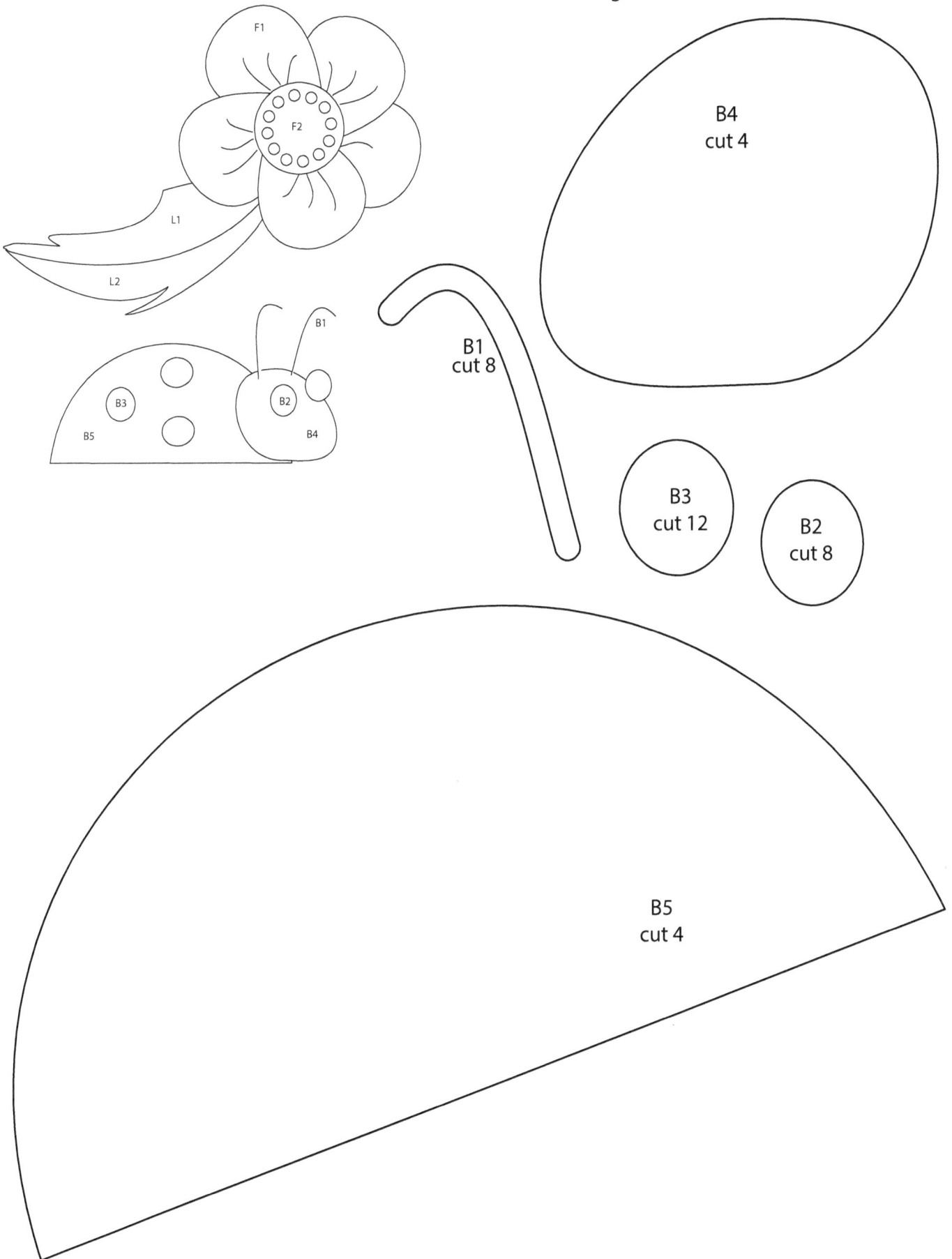

F1

F2

L1

L2

B1

B3

B2

B4

B5

B4
cut 4

B1
cut 8

B3
cut 12

B2
cut 8

B5
cut 4

L1
cut 5

L2
cut 5

F2
cut 5

F1
cut 25

In the "olden days" my father rode a horse to school, and helped in the South Texas family garden. When he retired he didn't buy acres of land, but bought enough land to continue the family tradition of a big garden.

Our children fondly recall spending time with my parents and helping Paw and Maw plant, weed, and water in that very garden.

So after purchasing our land, I knew one of the first things I needed was a garden. My parents didn't have livestock to keep away from the vegetables, thus no need for a fence or a gate. Not so with our place.

Fencing the 8,000 sq. ft. garden was an interesting experience for two inexperienced barbed wire fence builders. Once we got the barbed wire fence up, we realized it would keep the cows and donkeys out, but not the jackrabbits!

Did you know that deer are not the least bit concerned about a fence? No! They jump it and eat all the leaves from tomato plants. Just an FYI. :)

On to plan B. We needed some type of netting with a small mesh. That took a while putting up the mesh to cover 8,000 sq. ft. only to discover it kept out the large jackrabbits, but the bunnies had fun running through the mesh and enjoying the veggies! We learned to plant enough for them, and us.

We realized we needed a tractor for the garden, and cows. The tractor wasn't a big deal, we bought an old Ford 9N, 1940 something tractor. I had never been on one before, but instantly it became mine!

Buying cows was another story. We went to the livestock sale, another new experience city gals miss, and I bought 2 cows. The cadence of the auctioneer was tough to understand, but I succeeded. Of course, I could have gotten them cheaper had I not kept bidding against myself!

And, I got laughed out of the feed store when I went in and asked for feed the cows would love, so they would like us!

Learning to live "40 miles from nowhere" was a lot of trial and error. Mostly error! But fun!

One can't work in a large garden without a wheelbarrow and lots of gloves. I must admit, my wheelbarrow doesn't look exactly like the one for this month's block, but it does the job. I dressed this wheelbarrow up a bit for the quilt.

No garden would be complete without a scarecrow with a plaid shirt, jeans, an old hat and hay for arms and legs. We had a scarecrow cute enough for a quilt, but not this quilt. He is on another of our quilt designs.

Beyond the Gate

Beyond the Gate

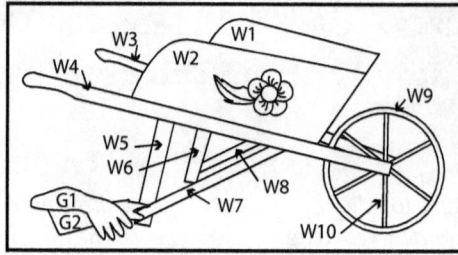

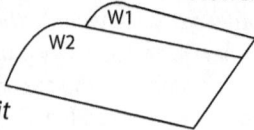

Gloves Unit   *Flower/Leaf Unit*

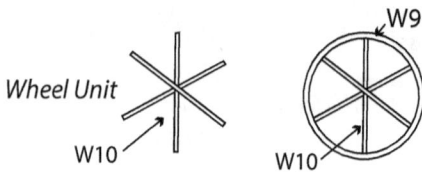

Bucket Unit

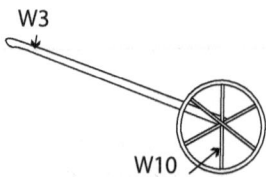

Wheel Unit

Back Handle Positioning

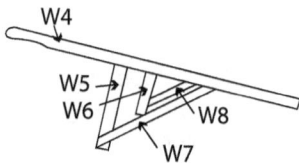

Front Handle/Legs Unit

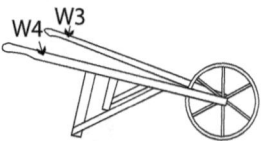

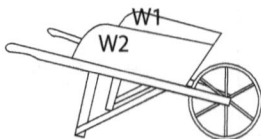

L1, L2, F1, F2 unit

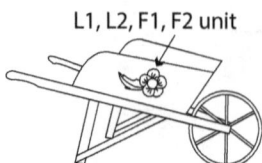

Complete the wheelbarrow

Fabric Requirements:

Block:
39" x 20 ½" gold

Applique:

flower	11" x 9"
flower centers	3" x 3"
light leaves	3" x 9"
medium leaves	3" x 9"
gloves	7" x 10"
wheel & spokes	11" x 12"
wheelbarrow structure [W3-8]	¼ yd.
bucket front	20" x 7"
bucket back	15" x 4"

Paper backed web (17"):
1 ½ yd.

Stabilizer:
To prevent fabric puckering, use your favorite type of stabilizer behind the appliqué pieces. Tear away stabilizer is a good choice for this purpose.

Thread:
Matching or contrasting thread, as you prefer.

Suggestion:
Use two different colors for the flower petals, one lighter than the other. Embellish the flower with embroidery thread.

For added emphasis, put long running stitches within each of the blocks.

Beyond the Gate

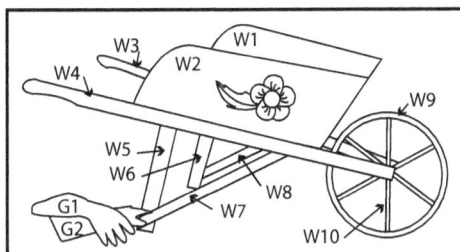

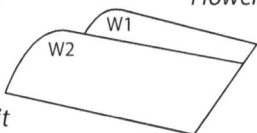

Gloves Unit   *Flower/Leaf Unit*

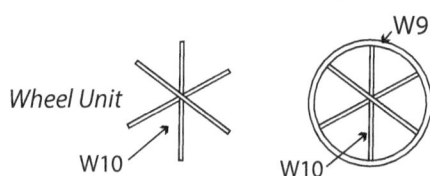

Bucket Unit

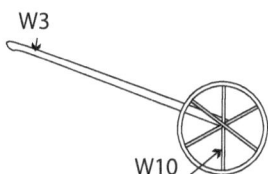

Wheel Unit

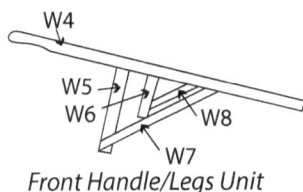

Back Handle Positioning

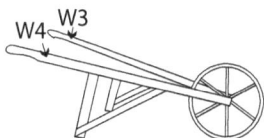

Front Handle/Legs Unit

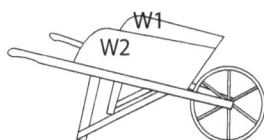

L1, L2, F1, F2 unit

Complete the wheelbarrow

Rotary Cutting
• Cut [1] background rectangle 39" x 20 ½"

Wheelbarrow, Gloves & Flower
• Trace applique pieces on the paper backed web material
• Press paper backed web to the wrong side of the applique fabric
• Cut out applique pieces

On a teflon or applique sheet:
• **Gloves Unit**
  • Place [G1] over [G2] allowing the fingers of the gloves to drape over [G1]
• **Flower Unit** (same instructions as for month 1, smaller size)
  • Create a flower unit by overlapping [5] petals
  • Place the center circle over the petals
  • Press
• **Leaf Unit** (same instructions as for month 1, smaller size)
  • Create a leaf unit by overlapping the light/dark pieces
  • Press
• **Wheelbarrow Unit**
  • *Bucket*
    • Place [W1] behind [W2], line up right edges
    • Press
  • *Wheel*
    • Arrange spokes [W10] evenly spaced, crossing in the center
    • Place wheel [W9] over spokes [W10]
    • Press
  • *Legs*
    • Place leg support [W7] over leg [W5], match lower left edge
    • Place leg support [W8] behind leg [W6], match lower left edge
  • *Complete the wheelbarrow*
    • Place back handle [W3] behind wheel [W9], angle as shown in layout
    • Place bucket unit over back handle, maintain angle
    • Place front handle [W4] & legs units over wheel unit and bucket unit, keep legs & wheel on same plane
    • Press all
    • Place flower/leaf unit over bucket unit, press

Complete the block
• Place the gloves unit over the wheelbarrow unit on the background fabric
• Press

Applique
• Use a tear away stabilizer behind each block and applique the edges using a blanket stitch, satin stitch, or close zig zag stitch

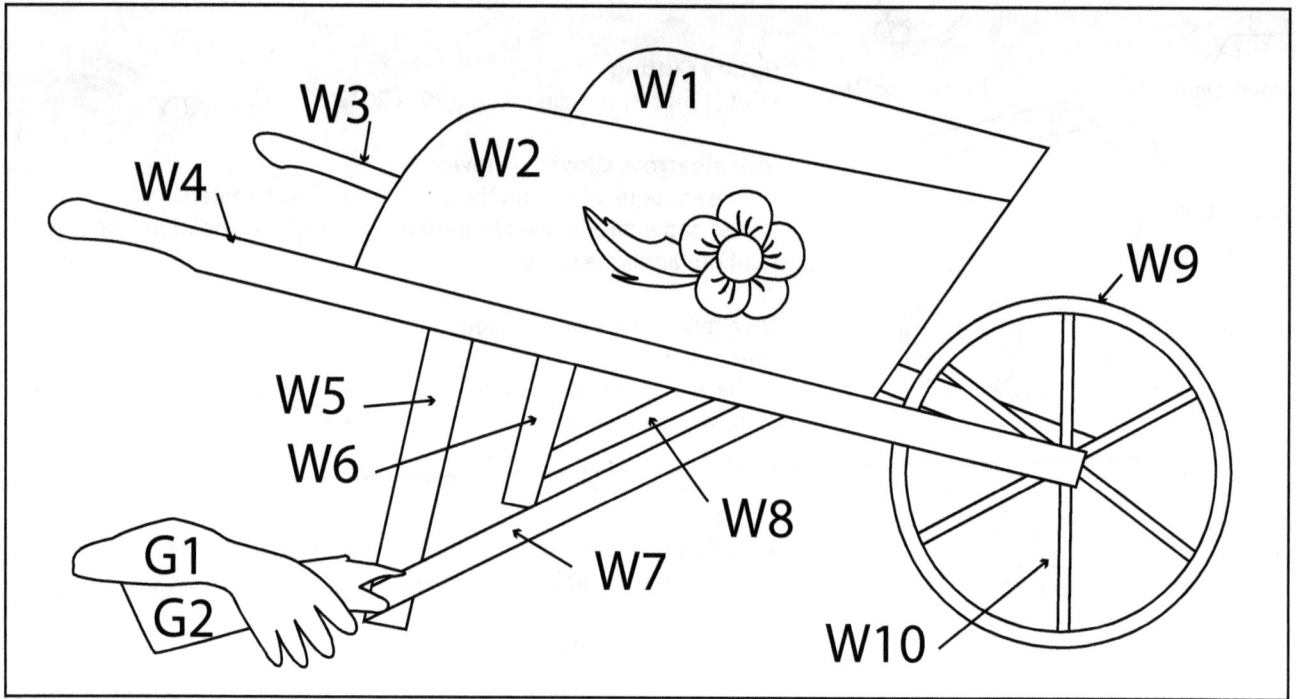

Pattern reversed for tracing

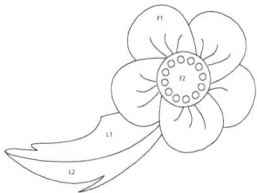

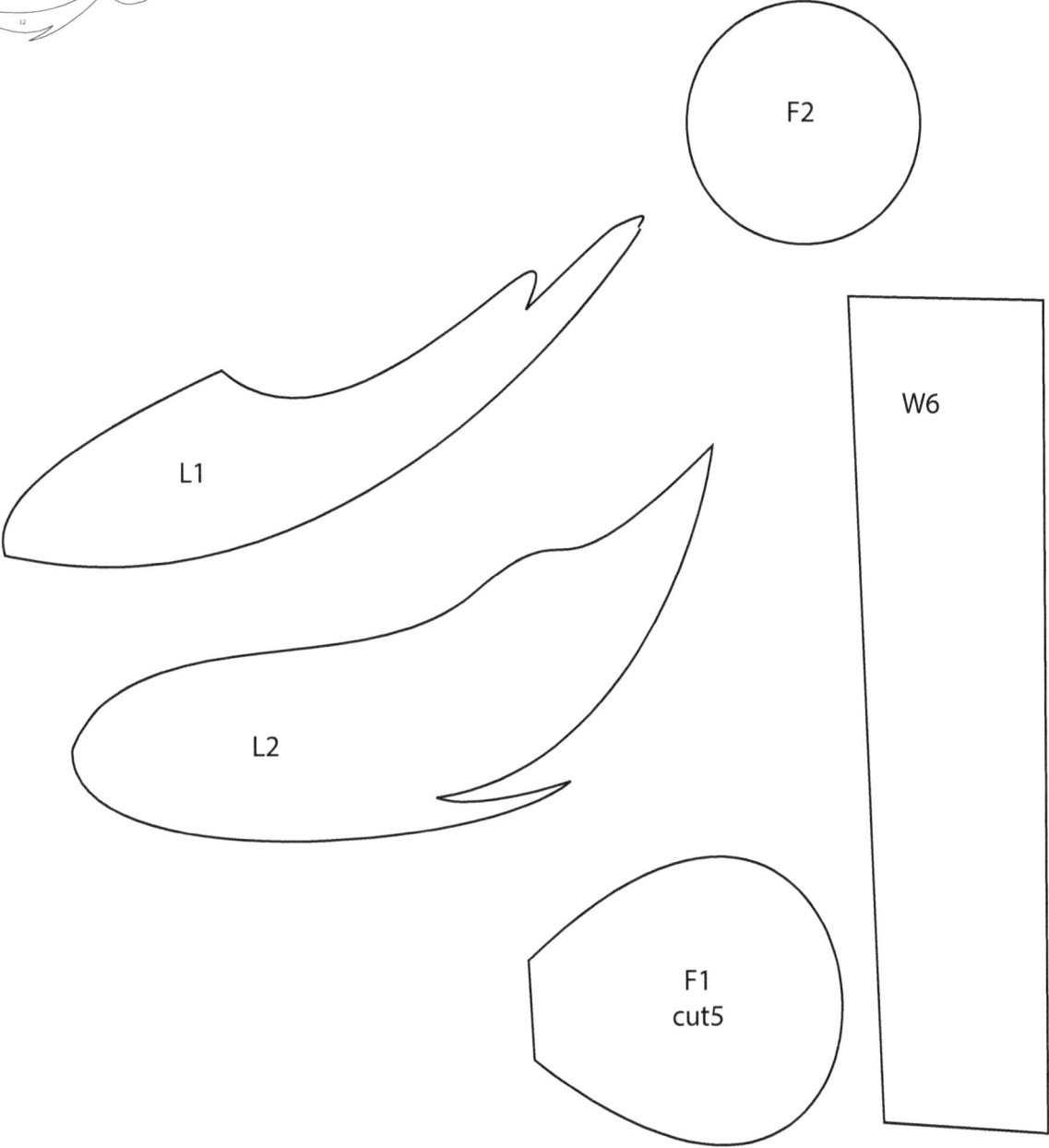

F2

W10
cut
3

L1

W6

L2

F1
cut5

17

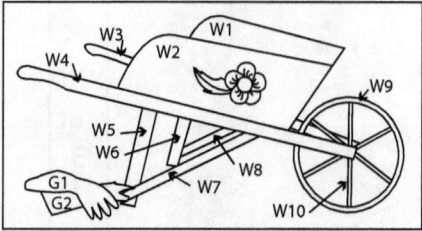

Pattern reversed for tracing

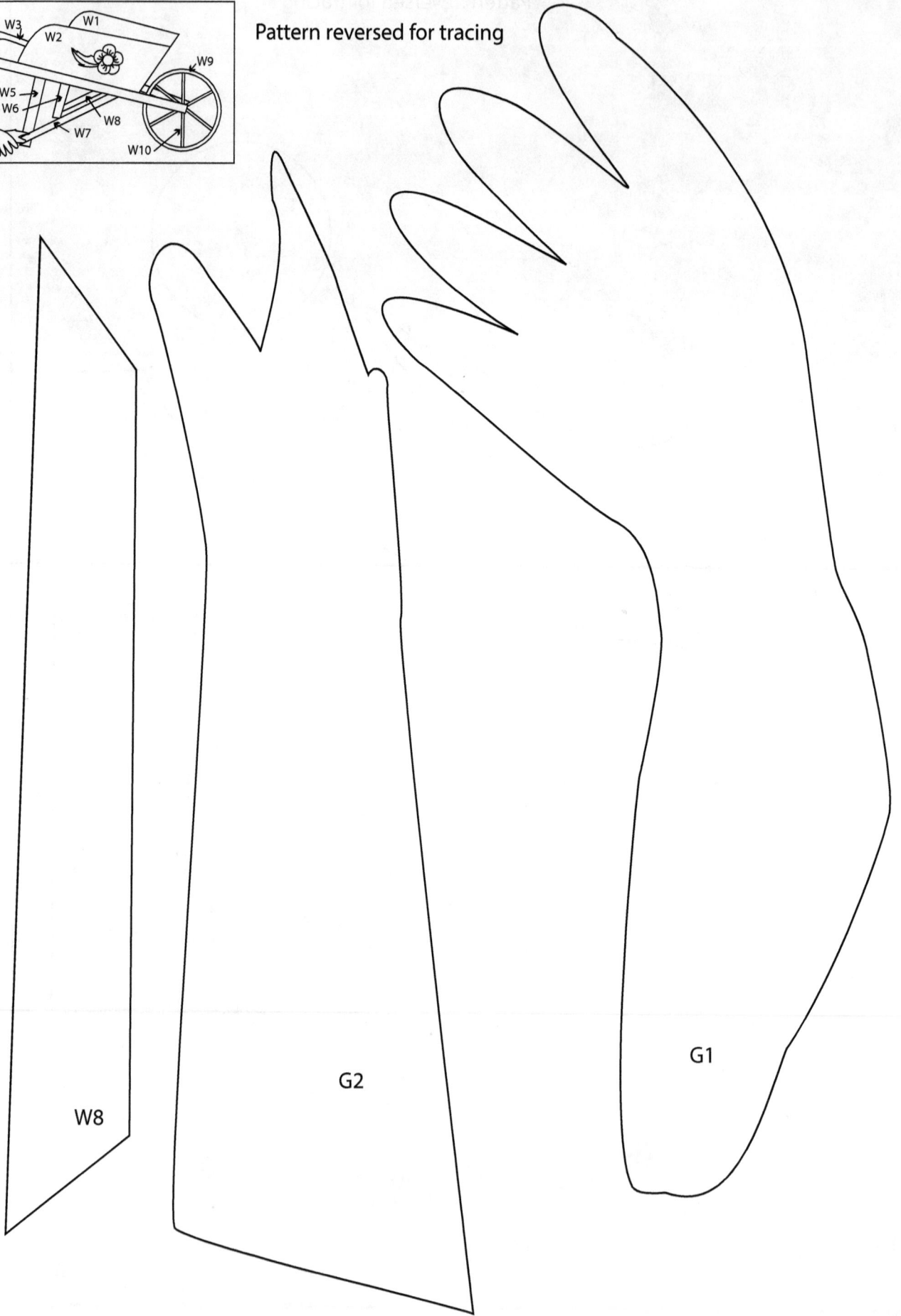

W3
W1
W4
W2
W5
W6
W9
G1
W8
G2
W7
W10

W8

G2

G1

18

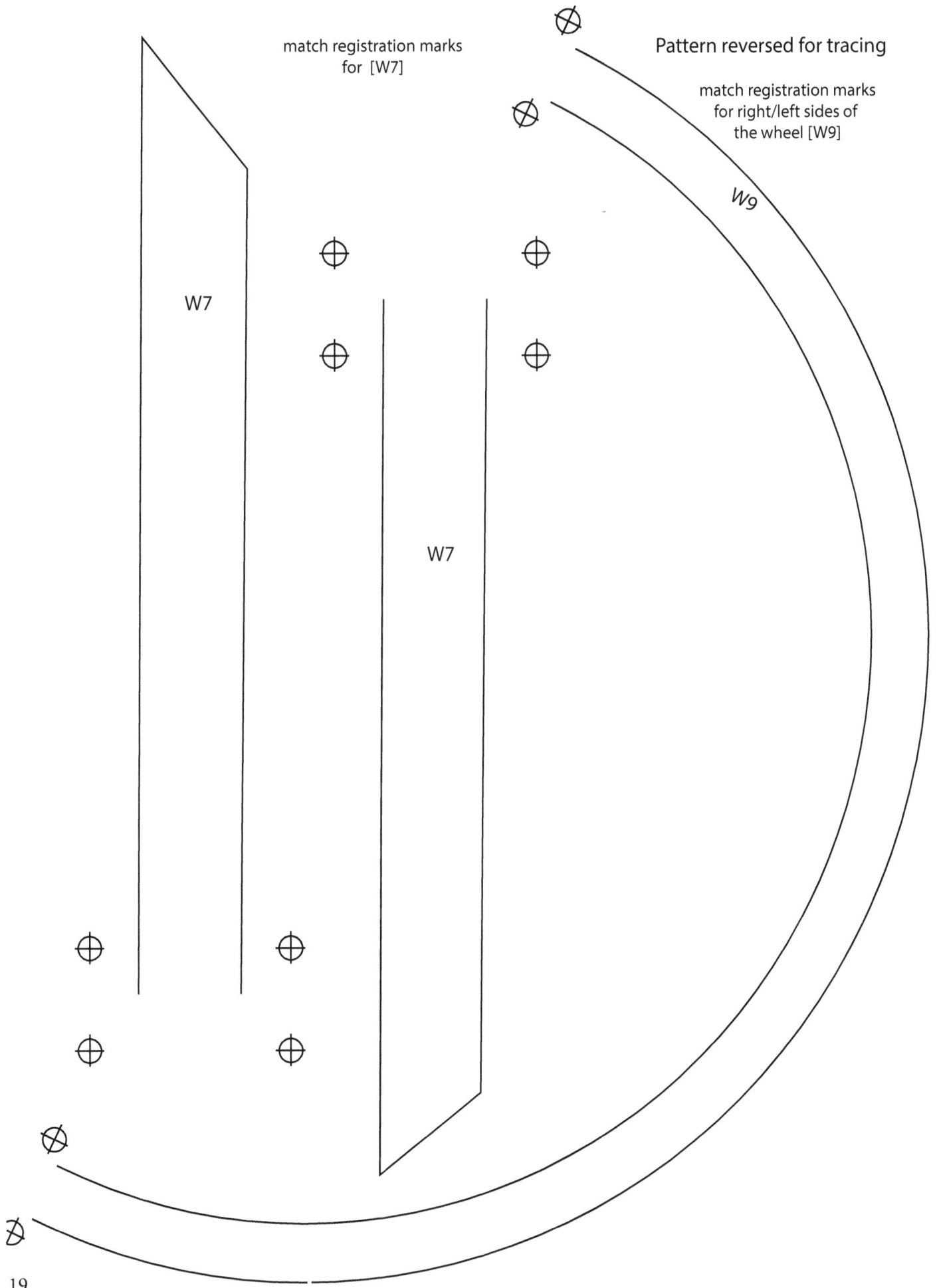

match registration marks
for [W7]

Pattern reversed for tracing

match registration marks
for right/left sides of
the wheel [W9]

W9

W7

W7

19

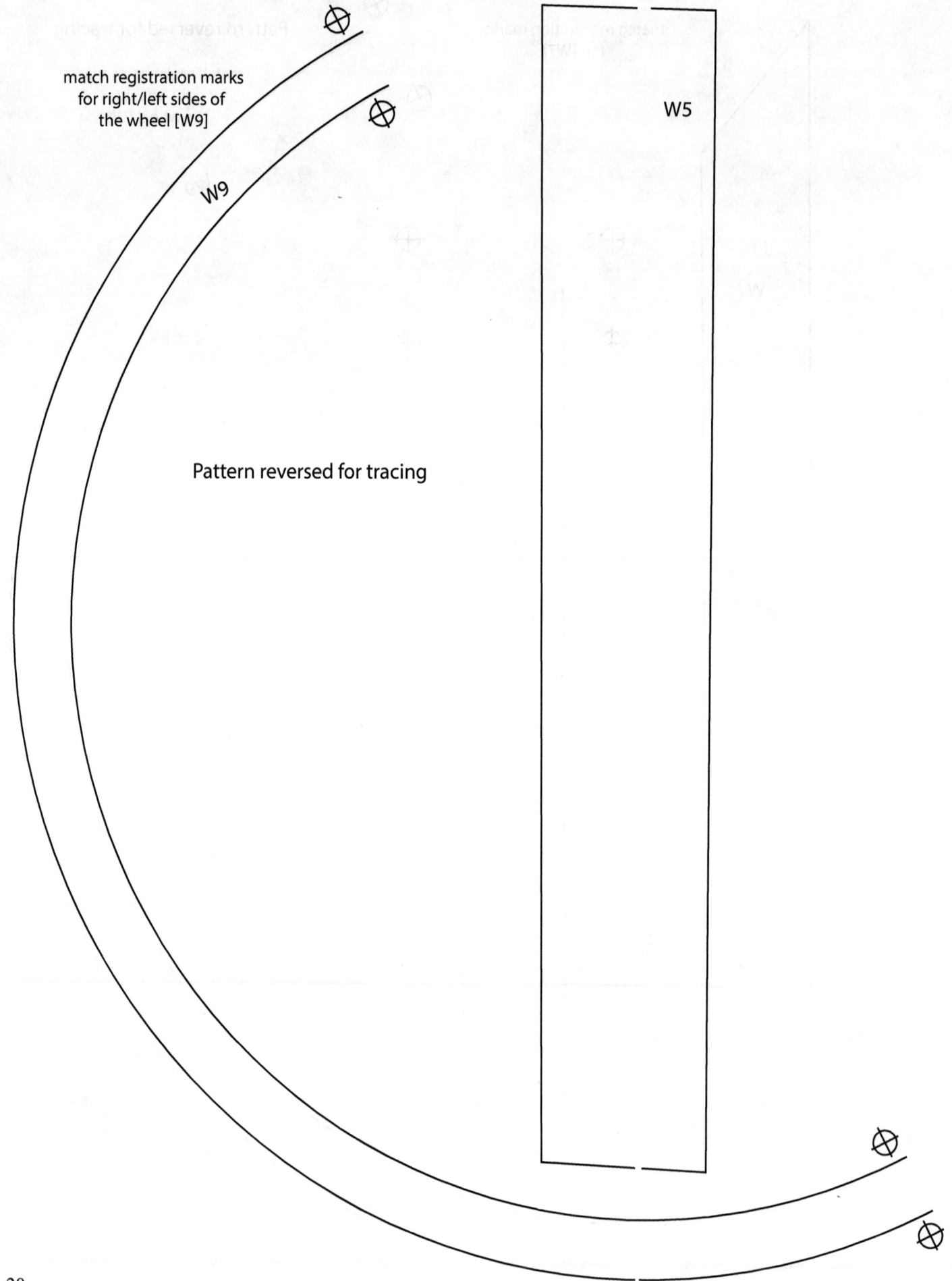

match registration marks
for right/left sides of
the wheel [W9]

W9

Pattern reversed for tracing

W5

match registration marks
for [W1]

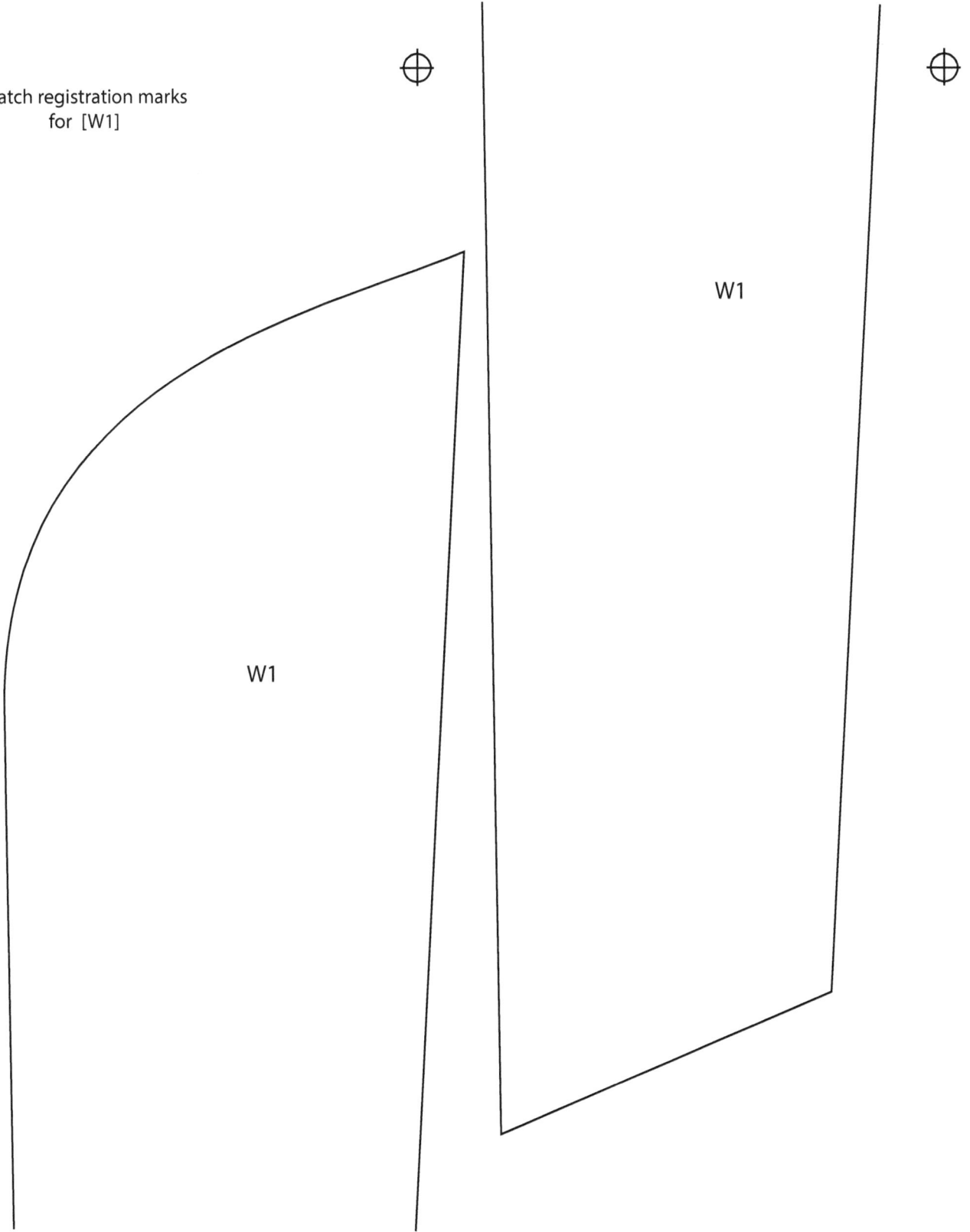

W1

W1

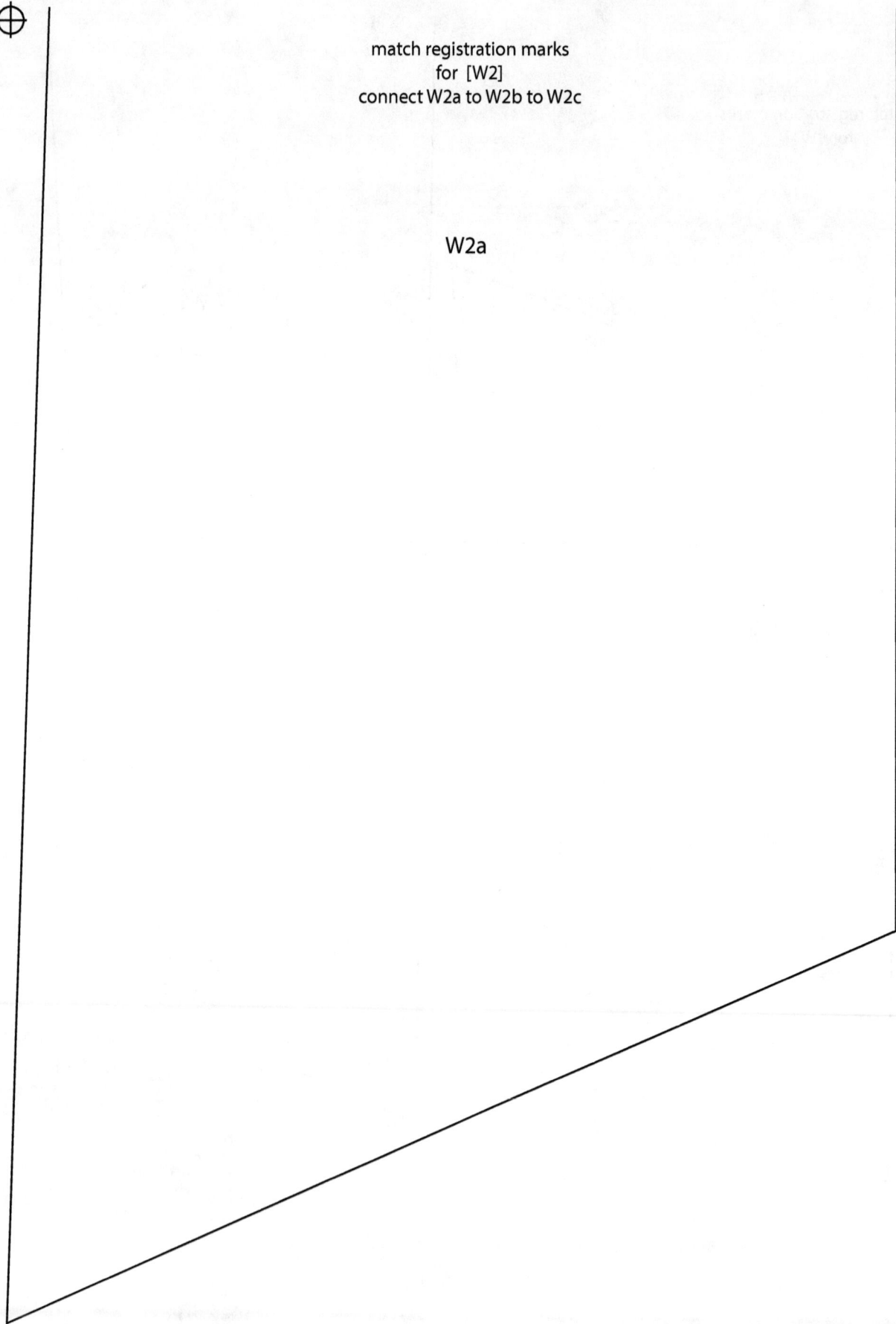

Pattern reversed for tracing

match registration marks
for [W2]
connect W2a to W2b to W2c

W2a

match registration marks
for [W2]
connect W2a to W2b to W2c
W2b is turned 90 degrees to fit the page.
When tracing, turn back 90 degrees.

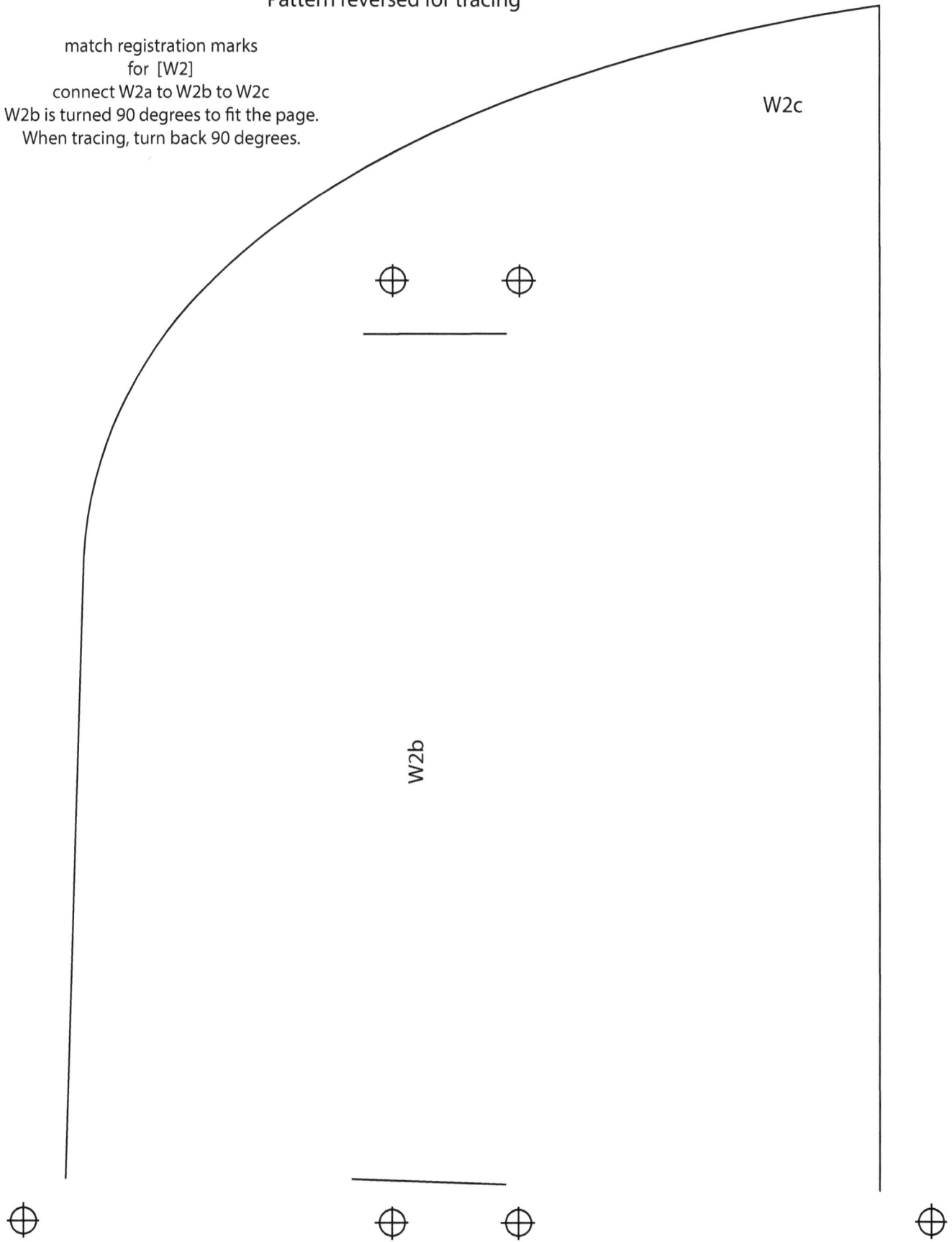

W2c

W2b

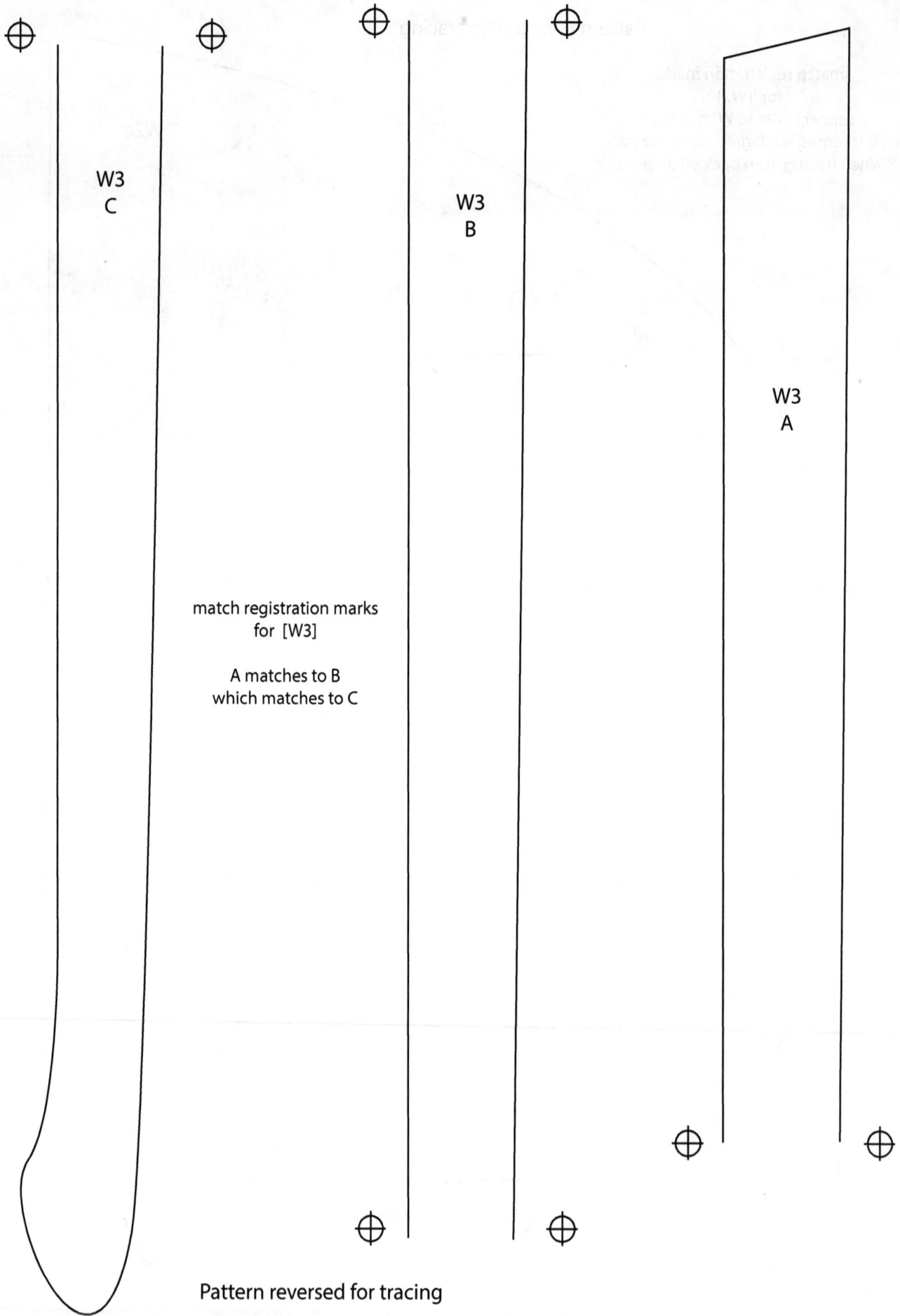

W3
C

W3
B

W3
A

match registration marks
for [W3]

A matches to B
which matches to C

Pattern reversed for tracing

Pattern reversed for tracing

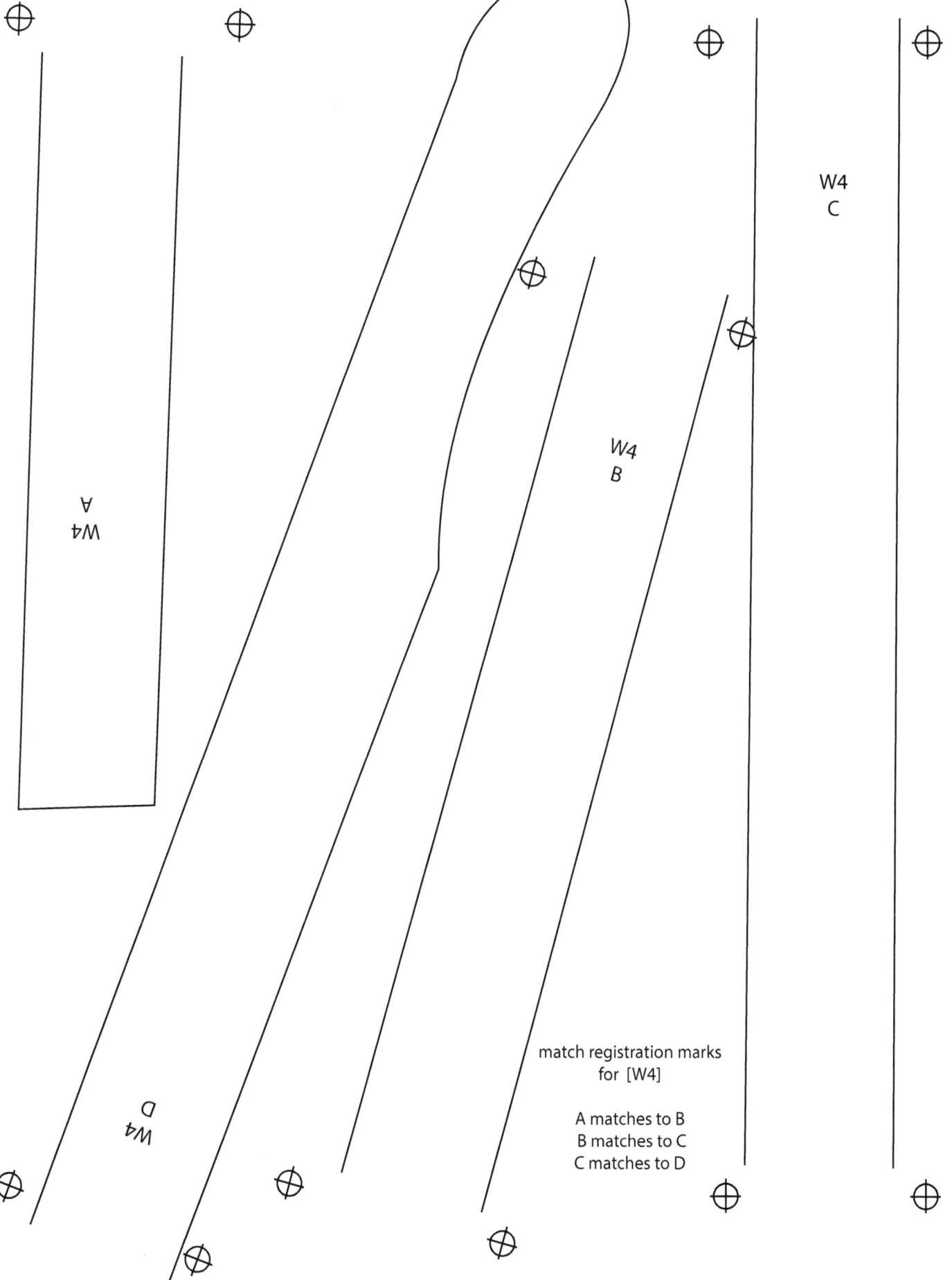

W4
C

W4
B

W4
A

W4
D

match registration marks
for [W4]

A matches to B
B matches to C
C matches to D

show & tell

Gates are quite important on a ranch. None of ours are quite this fancy with tulips adorning it, but we do have quite a few gates. Gates can be used to keep things out, or to keep things in. Hmmm...

Of course we have a gate to the garden. It has a chain and a u-shaped area for the chain to wrap around a pole and hook into. It didn't take long for the livestock to equate the chain clanging against the pole to be their signal they would get some veggies thrown over the fence to them.

When we first bought our property, we let the livestock graze everywhere, except the garden. That did present a few problems. They totally ate one of the battery operated large cars we had for our grandchildren. Not a small car, but the type the children drive!

One day I noticed something green inside a cow's mouth, only to find her eating a child's plastic golf club. When they started gnawing on the house...we put up another barbed wire fence and cattle guard. :)

A friend told us we should let our two heifers visit his ranch for a couple of months. First of all, I didn't even know we had heifers! Heifers are females that are beyond the calf stage, and haven't had any calves themselves. I thought we had cows! Nope...heifers become cows after they have a calf.

Plus, one of our heifers had horns! I thought only bulls had horns. More learning experiences, "40 miles from nowhere".

The herd began to increase, and increase until one of the calves was a bull calf. That presented a problem. To make a long story short, with one rubber band I turned a bull calf into a steer. Enough said.

More livestock, more fences and more gates. Much like the wheelbarrow block, I embellished the gate for this block more than one of our gates. Critters are beautiful in their own right, but they eat flowers and anything else in sight.

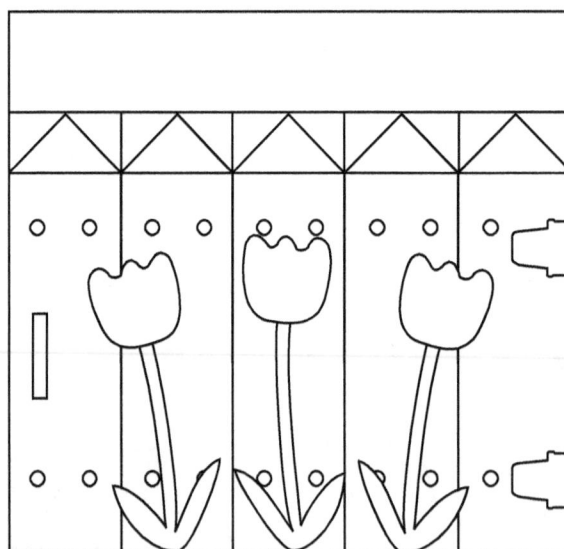

Beyond the Gate

Beyond the Gate

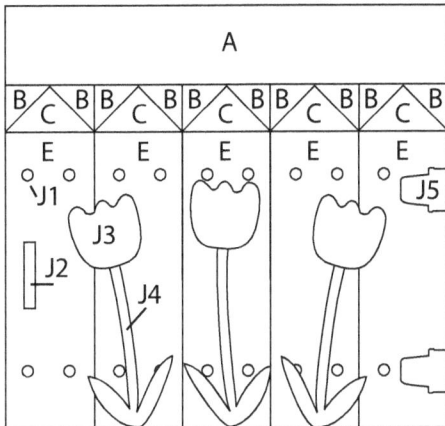

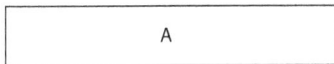

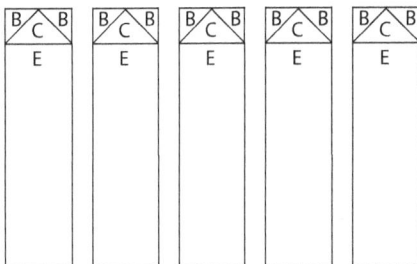

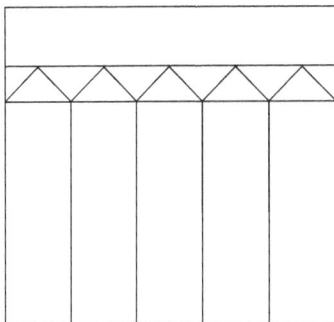

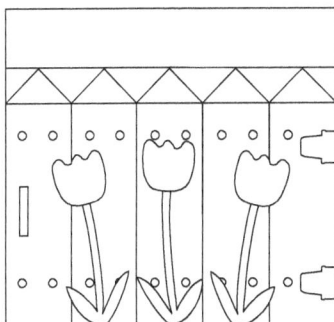

Fabric Requirements:

Blocks:
1 ½ yd. light purple
½ yd. dark purple

Applique:
tulips	21" x 8"
stem/leaves	18" x 20"
gate handle	2" x 6"
gate hinges	5" x 10"
nails	5" x 6"

Paper backed web (17"):
1 ¼ yd.

Stabilizer:
To prevent fabric puckering, use your favorite type of stabilizer behind the appliqué pieces. Tear away stabilizer is a good choice for this purpose.

Thread:
Matching or contrasting thread, as you prefer.

Suggestions:
For added emphasis, put long running stitches within each of the blocks.

Or, perhaps stitch butterflies in the solid block above the fence.

Beyond the Gate

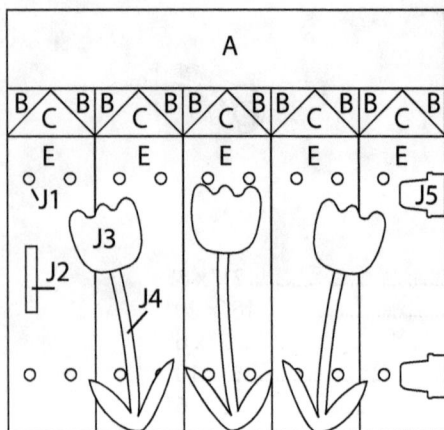

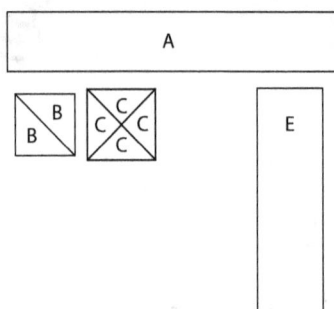

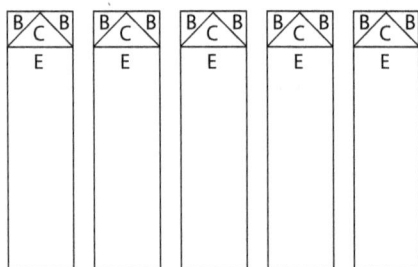

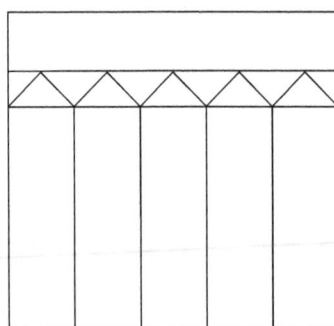

Rotary Cutting
- Cut [1] rectangle [A] 40 ½" x 7 ½"
- Cut [5] rectangles [E] 26 ½" x 8 ½"
- Cut [2] squares [C] 9 ¼", then cut [5] quarter square triangles [C]
- Cut [5] squares [B] 4 ⅞", then cut [10] half square triangles [B]

B/C/D Unit
- Stitch half square triangles [B] to [C]
- Press to dark fabric

E Unit
- Stitch each [B / C] unit to [E]
- Stitch [5] each [B/ C/ E] unit along the 26 ½" edge, press

Attach Units
- Stitch [A] to [B / C / E] unit, press

Applique Pieces
- Trace applique pieces on the paper backed web material
- Press paper backed web to the wrong side of the applique fabric
- Cut out applique pieces

On a teflon or applique sheet:
- **Flower Unit**
  - Create a flower unit by placing [J3] over [J4]
  - Press
  - Repeat the process for [2] more flowers

Complete the block
- Place the [4]nails on each fence board, line up nails using a ruler
- Press
- Place handle [J2] on left fence board
- Place [2]hinges [J5] on right fence board
- Press

Applique
- Use a tear away stabilizer behind each block and applique the edges using a blanket stitch, satin stitch, or close zig zag stitch

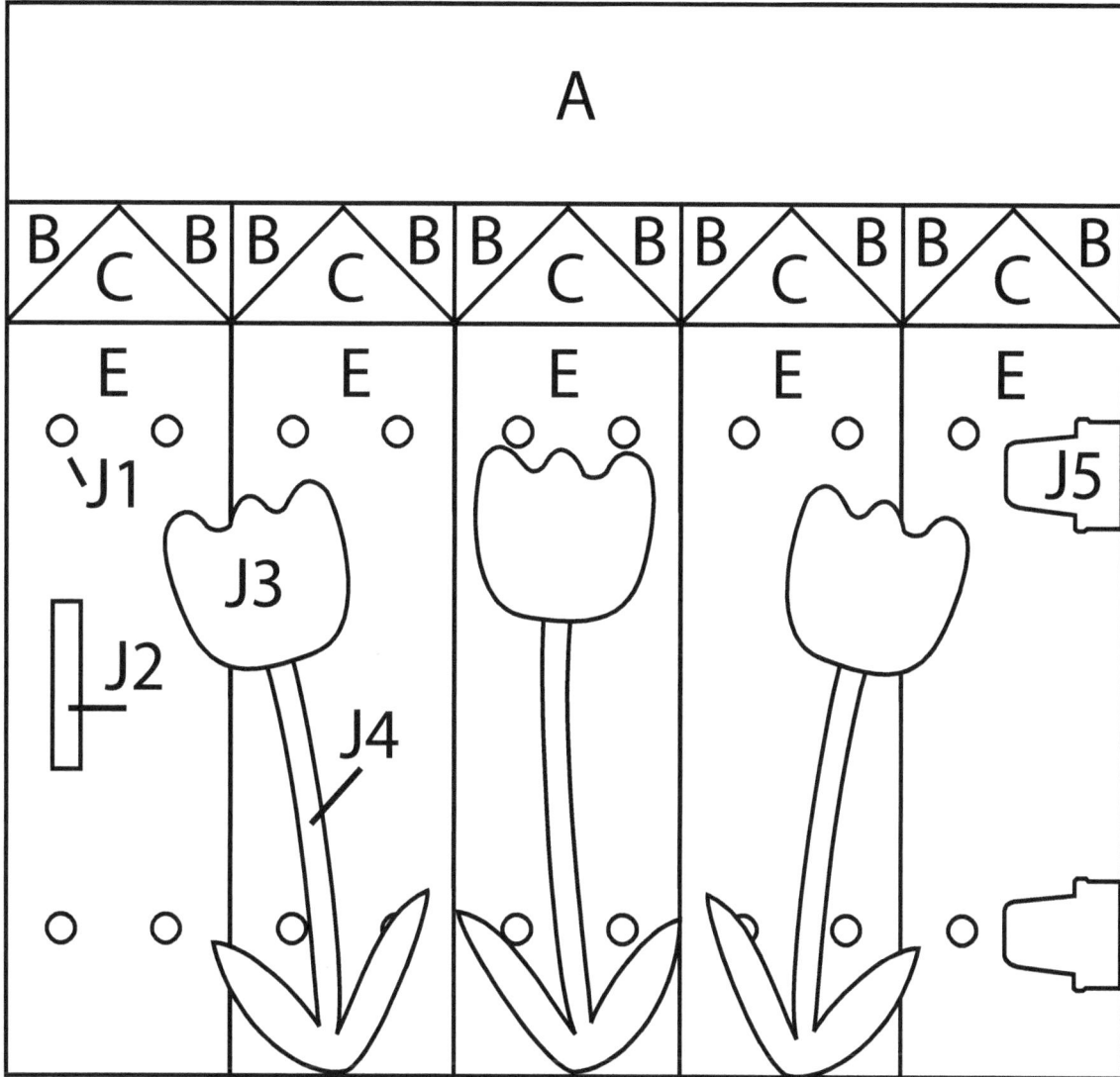

Pattern reversed for tracing

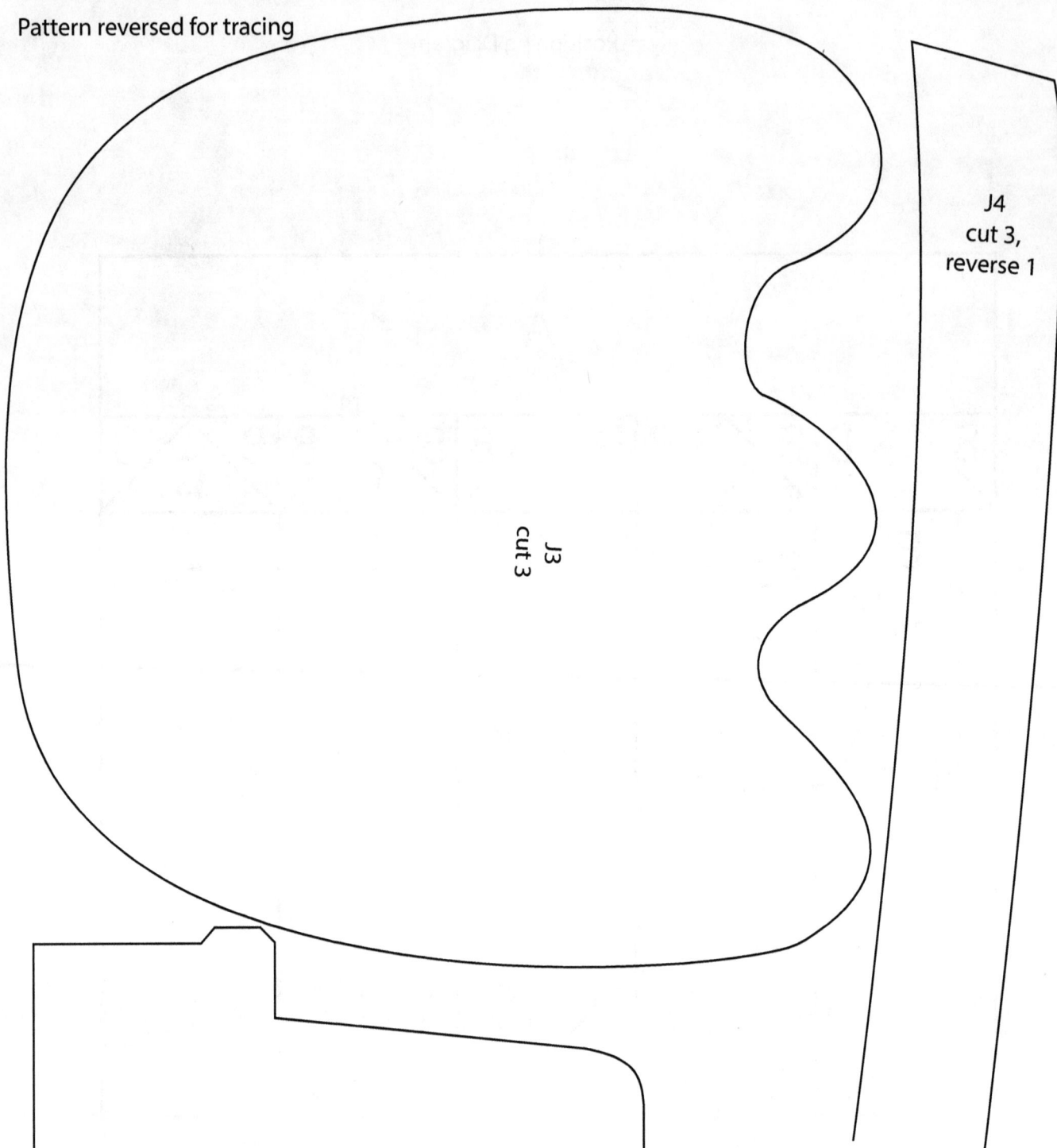

J4
cut 3,
reverse 1

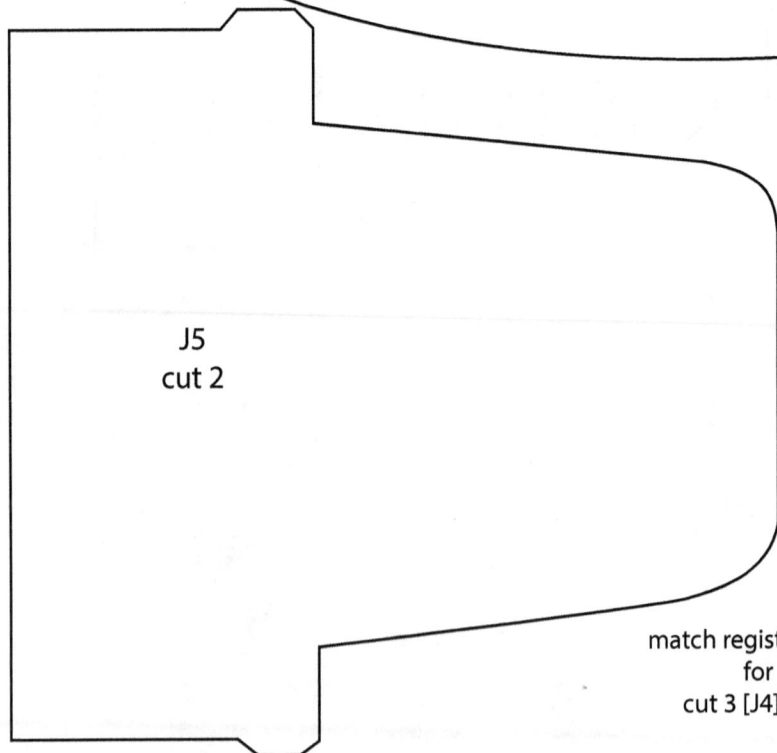

J3
cut 3

J5
cut 2

match registration marks
for [J4]
cut 3 [J4] reverse 1

Pattern reversed for tracing

J2

J4
cut 3
reverse 1

match registration marks
for [J4]

cut 2 [J4] and
flip the page to trace
one [J4] to face the
opposite direction

for a total of [3] stems/leaves [J4]

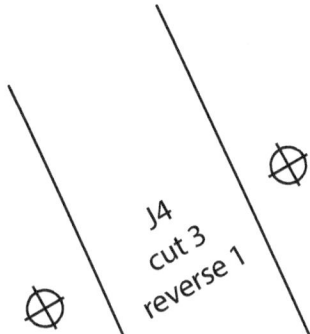

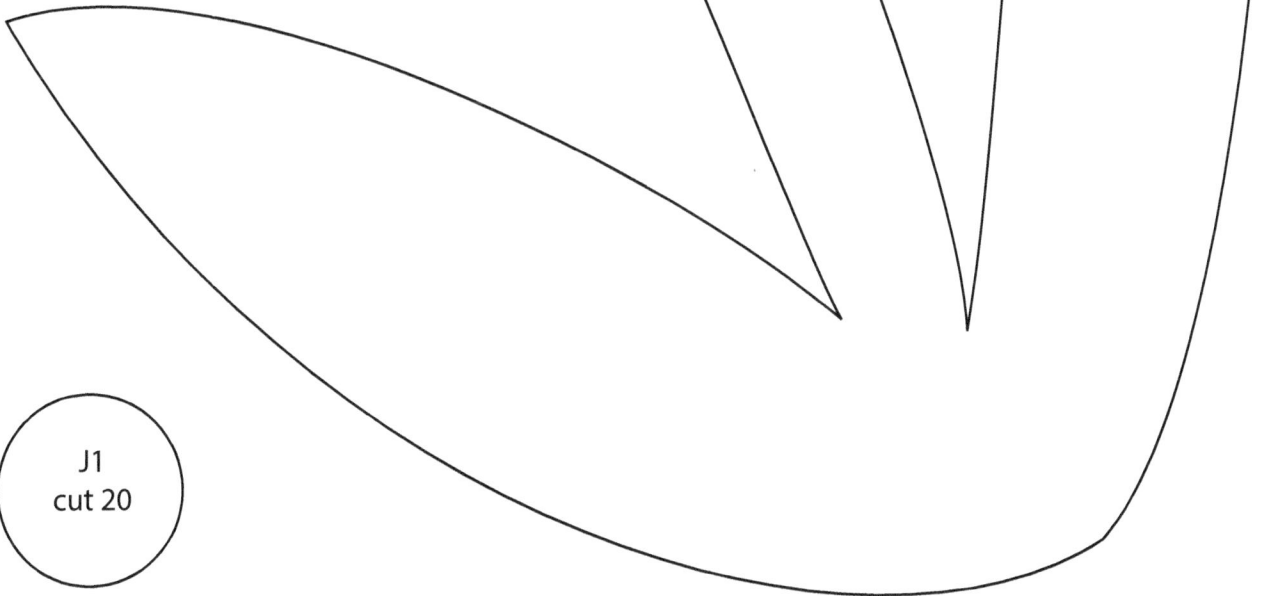

J1
cut 20

show & tell

Windmills are common place on a ranch, but this one holds special meaning to me. It's not one of those really tall, working windmills, but a beauty in its own right.

My husband put it together, painted it and placed it in a prominent area as you enter our property. We both wanted a windmill, thinking we would find one of the really large ones; but that wasn't the case.

One day I received a phone call from my sister letting me know she was sending me her most prized possession. I had no idea what her prized possession was, and why she would be sending it to me!

That's all she told me. No explanations, nothing.

She resides in a northern state, in an area with a typical housing arrangement. I live in a southern state, on a ranch, "40 miles from nowhere" .

On one of her trips to our southern state to visit our parents, she commented on a windmill...and so our father bought one and sent it to her. She had no where to put it, and kept the gift boxed up in her garage for years until the right time, and place.

It needed a home..."40 miles from nowhere".

Beyond the Gate

Beyond the Gate

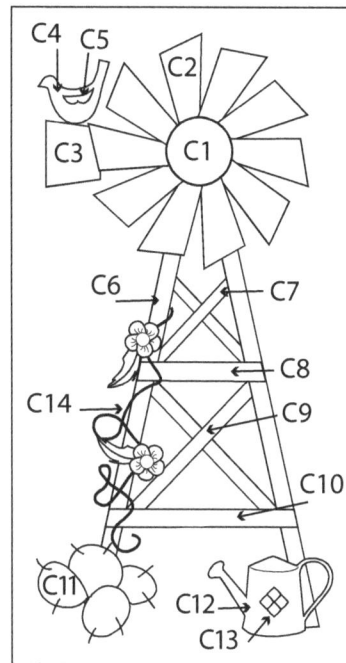

Fabric Requirements:

Block:
35 ½" x 66 ½" purple

Applique:

flower	12" x 9"
flower centers	2" x 2"
light leaves	4" x 6"
medium leaves	4" x 6"
windmill center	8" x 8"
windmill blades	28" x 17"
windmill frame [C6-C10]	52" x 11"
watering can	14" x 9"
watering can 4 square	3" x 3" ea.
vine	29" x 12"
cacti	9" x 18"
vane	8" x 14"
bird	9" x 8"
bird wing	2" x 4"

Paper backed web (17"):
2 ¾ yd.

Stabilizer:
To prevent fabric puckering, use your favorite type of stabilizer behind the appliqué pieces. Tear away stabilizer is a good choice for this purpose.

Thread:
Matching or contrasting thread, as you prefer.

Suggestion:
Use two different colors for the flower petals, one lighter than the other. Embellish the flower with embroidery thread.

For added emphasis, put long running stitches within each of the blocks.

Beyond the Gate

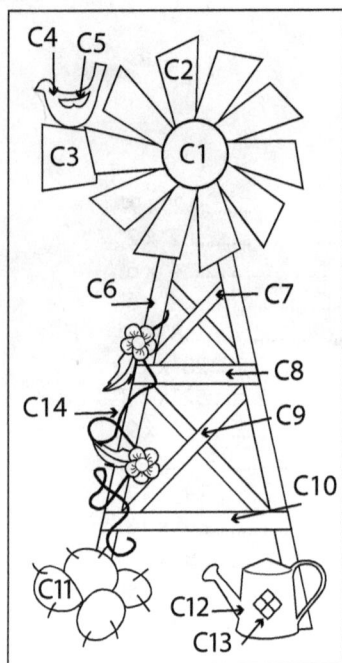

Rotary Cutting
- Cut [1] background rectangle 35½" x 66 ½"
  OR cut [2] 33½" x 35½", sew together along 33½" edge

Windmill
- Trace applique pieces on the paper backed web material
- Press paper backed web to the wrong side of the applique fabric
- Cut out applique pieces

On background fabric:
- **Frame Unit** (place bottom legs [C6] about 5-6" from bottom edge & slightly off center to the right to allow for the weather vane)
  - [C8] & [C10] control width of frame unit
  - Layout [2] [C6] pieces (angled ends at bottom - parallel to bottom edge), place [C8] over [C6]
  - Width of [C8] also controls vertical position
  - Place [C10] over [C6] pieces
  - Place [2] [C7] frame pieces to form an "x" behind [C6] for top frame support
  - Place [2] [C9] frame pieces to form an "x" behind [C6] for bottom frame support

On a teflon or applique sheet (or background):
- **Blade Unit**
  - Place [10] blades [C2] in a circular layout, be certain blade placement will cover tops of frame unit [C6] pieces
  - Place circle [C1] over center of blades, press
  - Place vane [C3] behind blades, press

- **Flower Unit** (same instructions as for month 1, smaller size)
  - Create a flower unit by overlapping [5] petals [F1] in a circular shape
  - Place the center circle [F2] over the petals, press
  - Repeat the process for [4] more petals

- **Leaf Unit** (same instructions as for month 1, smaller size)
  - Create a leaf unit by overlapping the light/dark pieces, press
  - Repeat the process for [4] more petals

- **Cactus Unit**
  - Place [4] cacti pieces [C11] in an irregular pattern, press

- **Watering Can Unit**
  - Place [4] square pieces [C13] on point on the watering can [C12], press

Complete the block
- Place frame unit on background
- Place blades unit over frame unit
- Place bird [C4] & [C5] on weather vane [C3]
- Place cacti unit at base of frame unit (left side)
- Place watering can unit at base of frame unit (right side)
- Place vine [C14] over frame unit
- Place flowers/leaf units over vine
- When all pieces are positioned, press

Applique
- Use a tear away stabilizer behind each block and applique the edges using a blanket stitch, satin stitch, or close zig zag stitch
- Threadpaint top of watering can

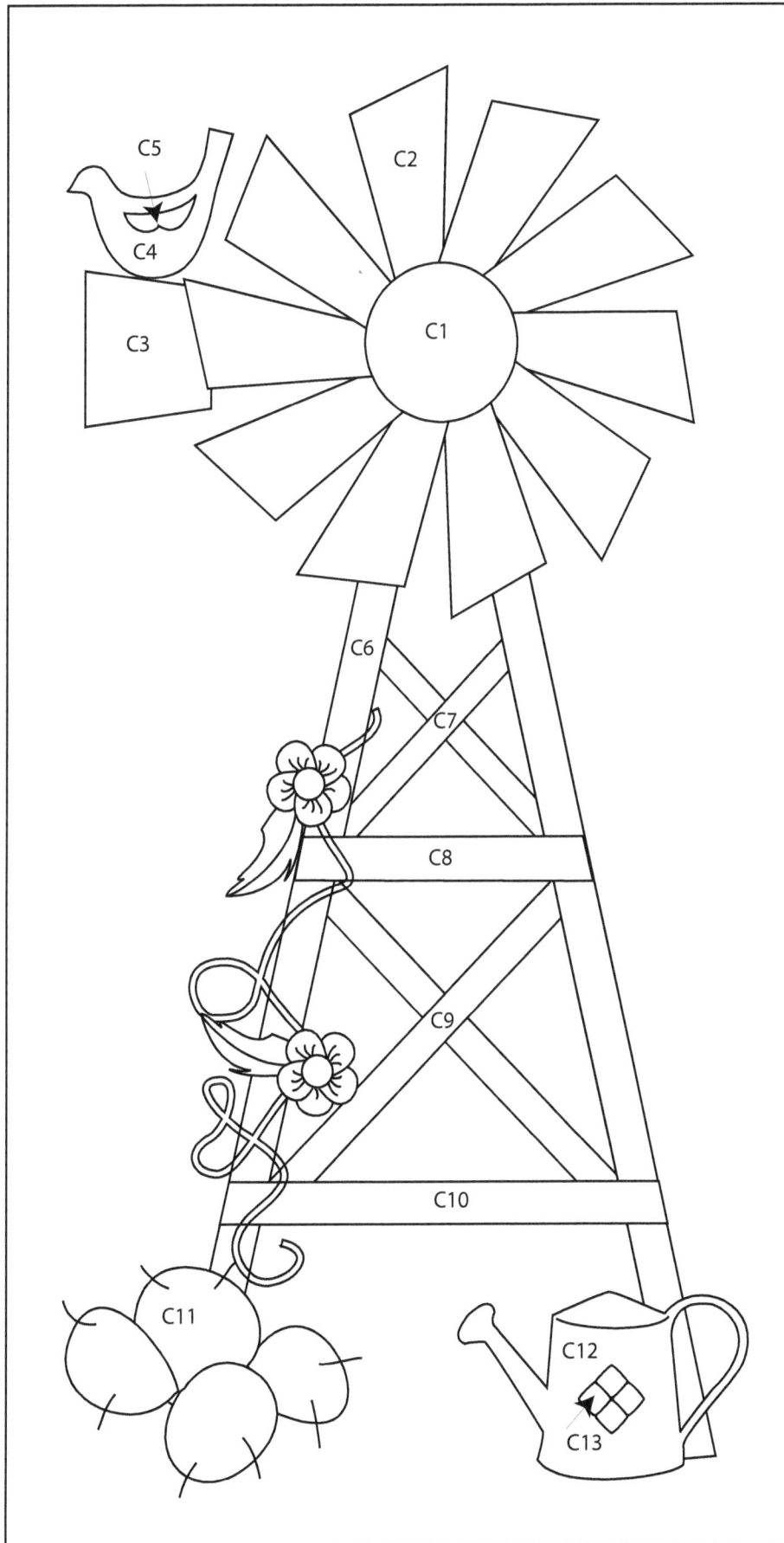

C5
C2
C4
C3
C1
C6
C7
C8
C9
C10
C11
C12
C13

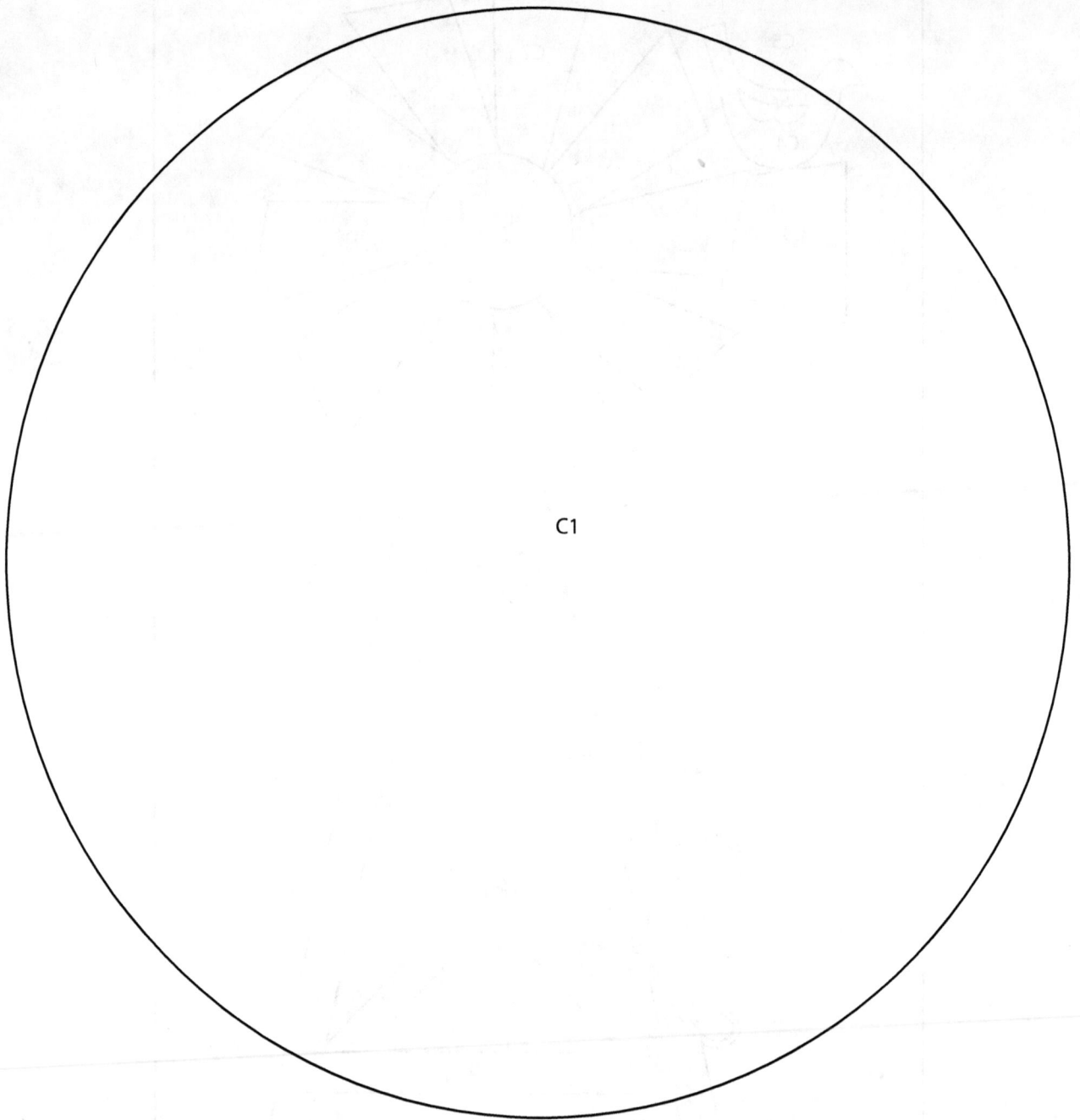

C1

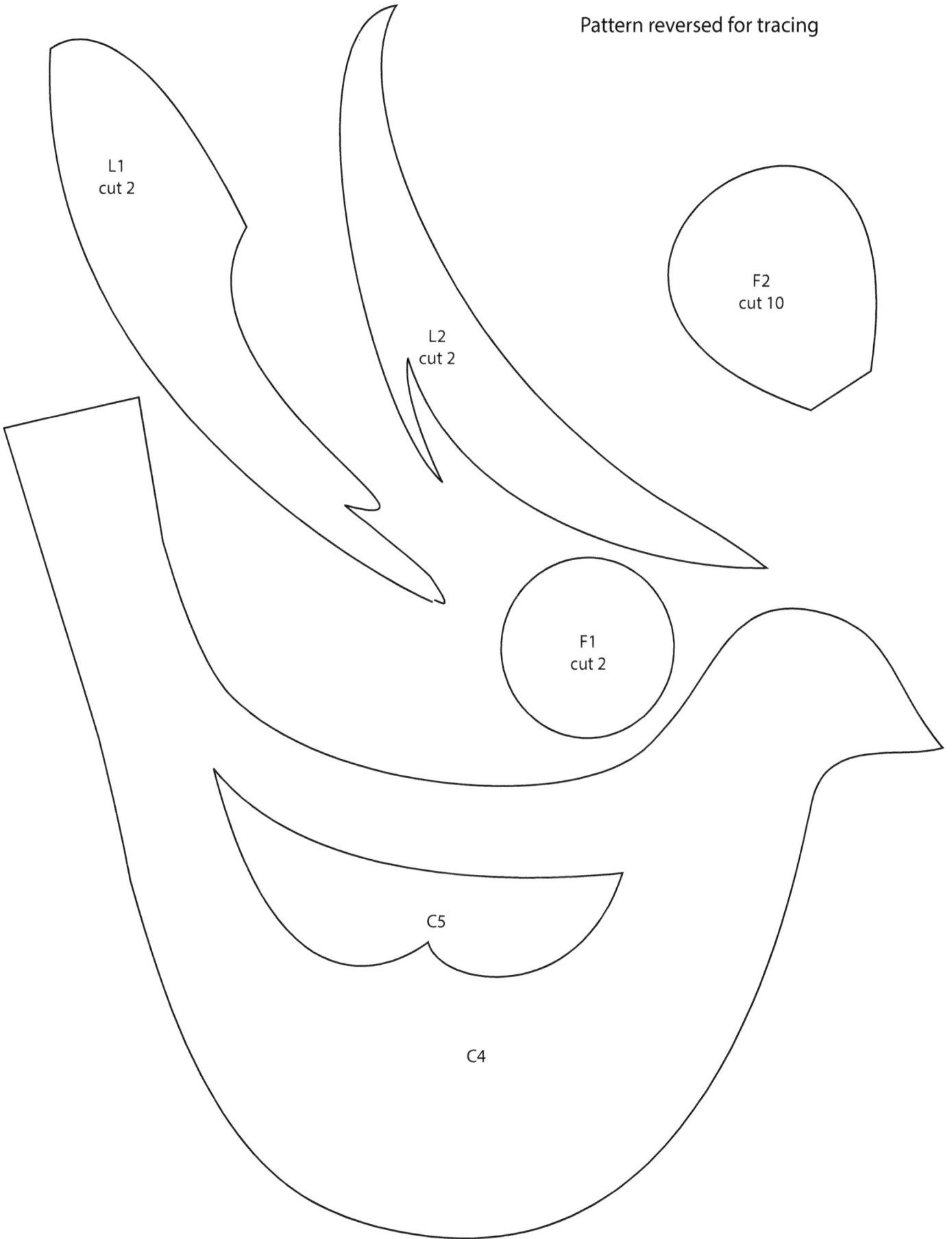

L1
cut 2

L2
cut 2

F2
cut 10

F1
cut 2

C5

C4

Pattern reversed for tracing

use registration marks to
match C2 to
C2 and trace
cut 10

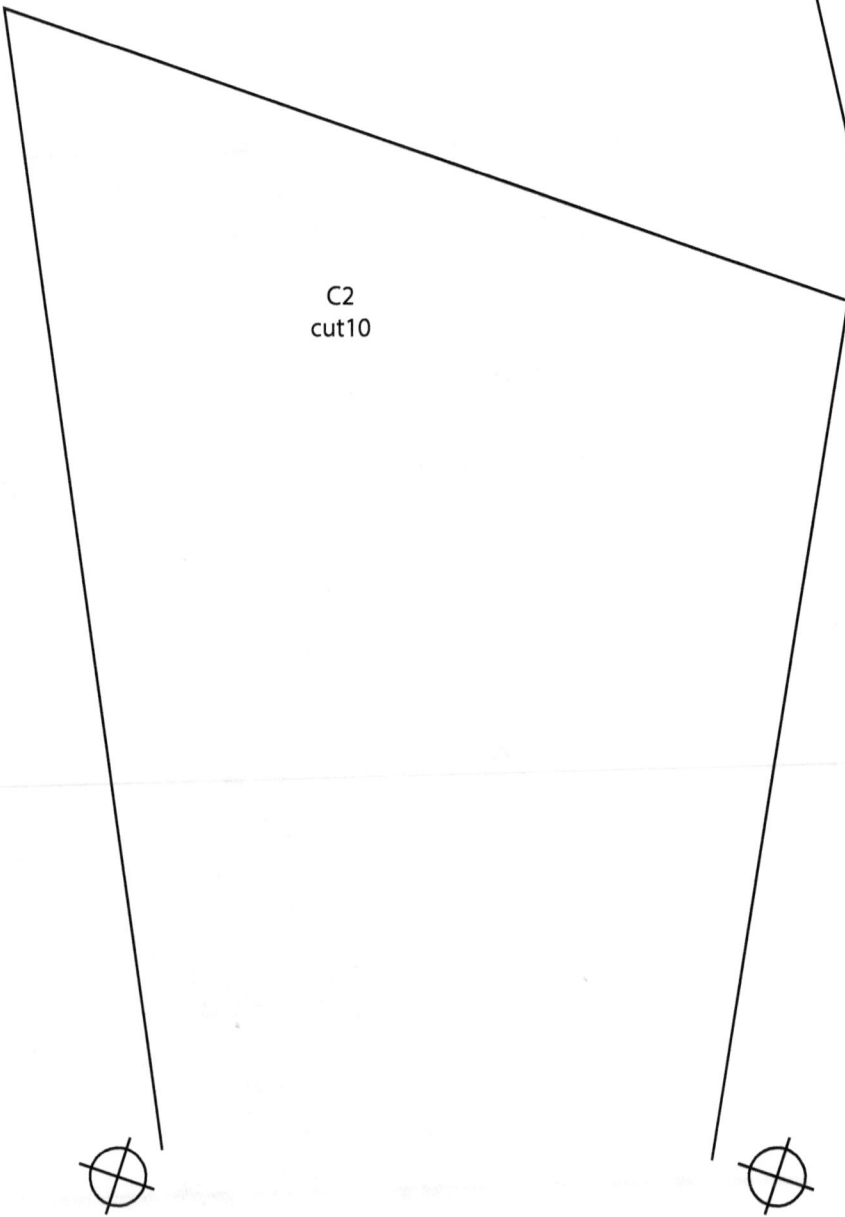

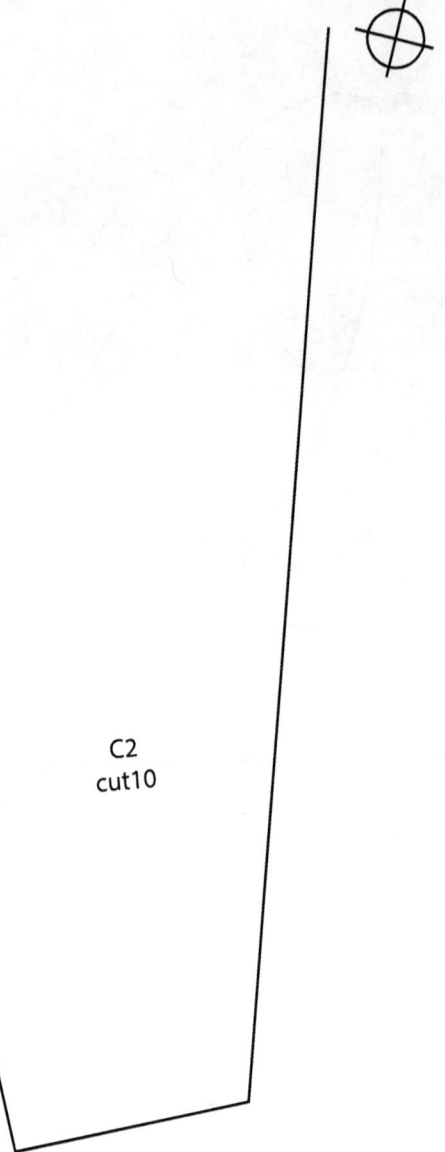

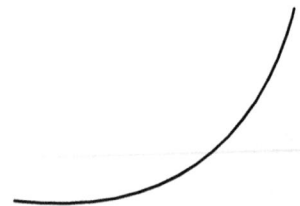

C2
cut10

C2
cut10

Threadpaint spikes on cacti

38

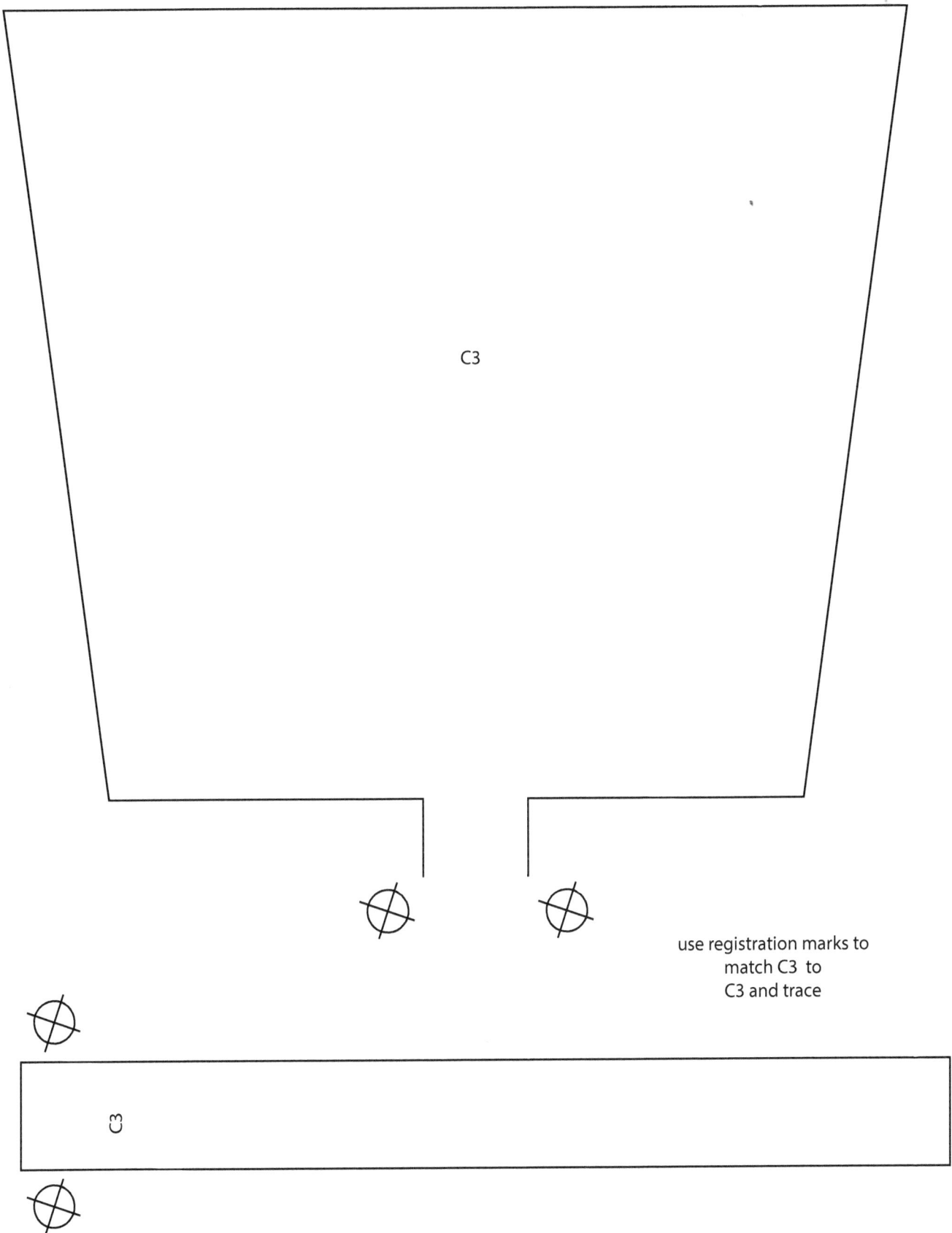

C3

use registration marks to
match C3 to
C3 and trace

C3

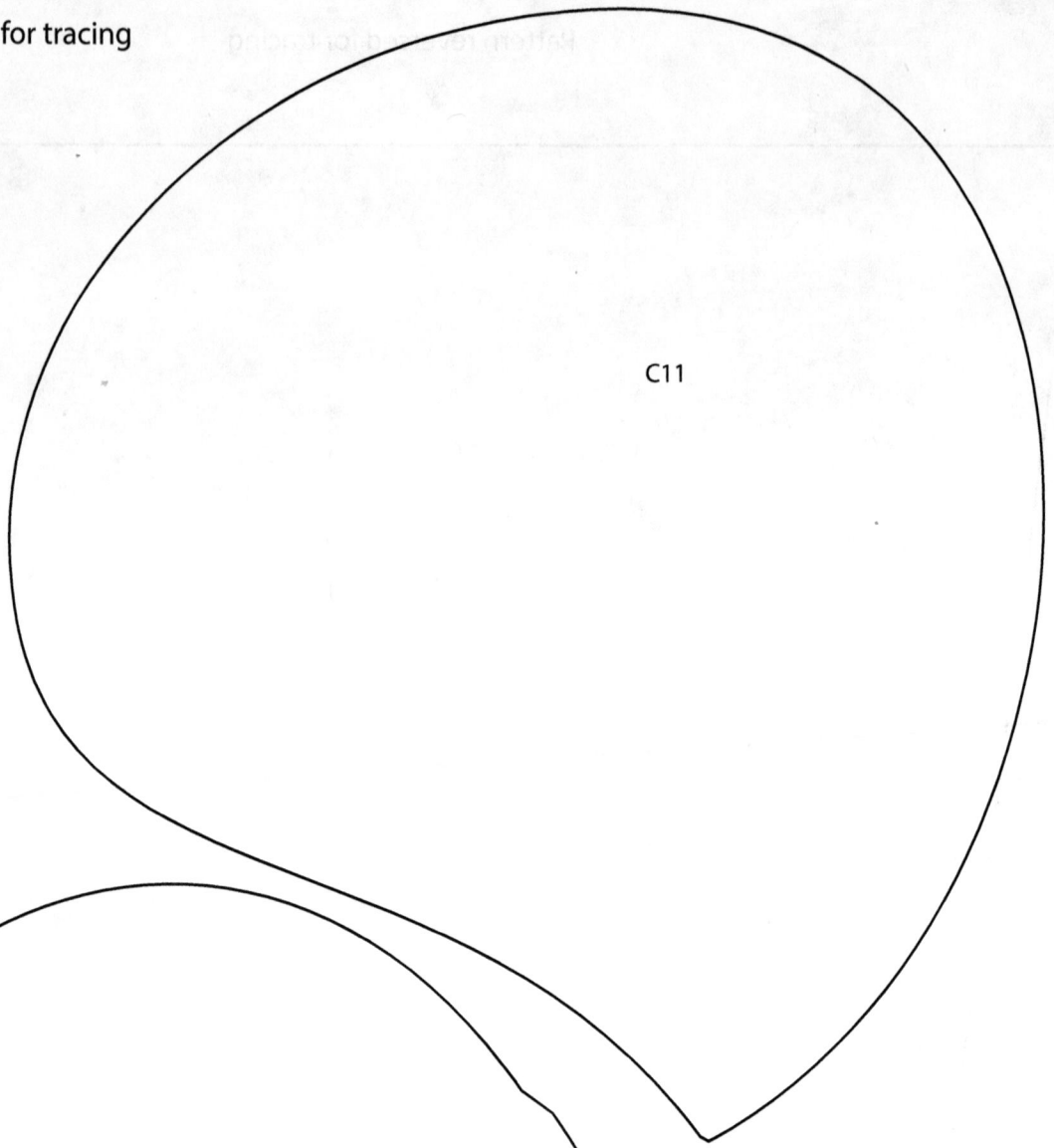

C11

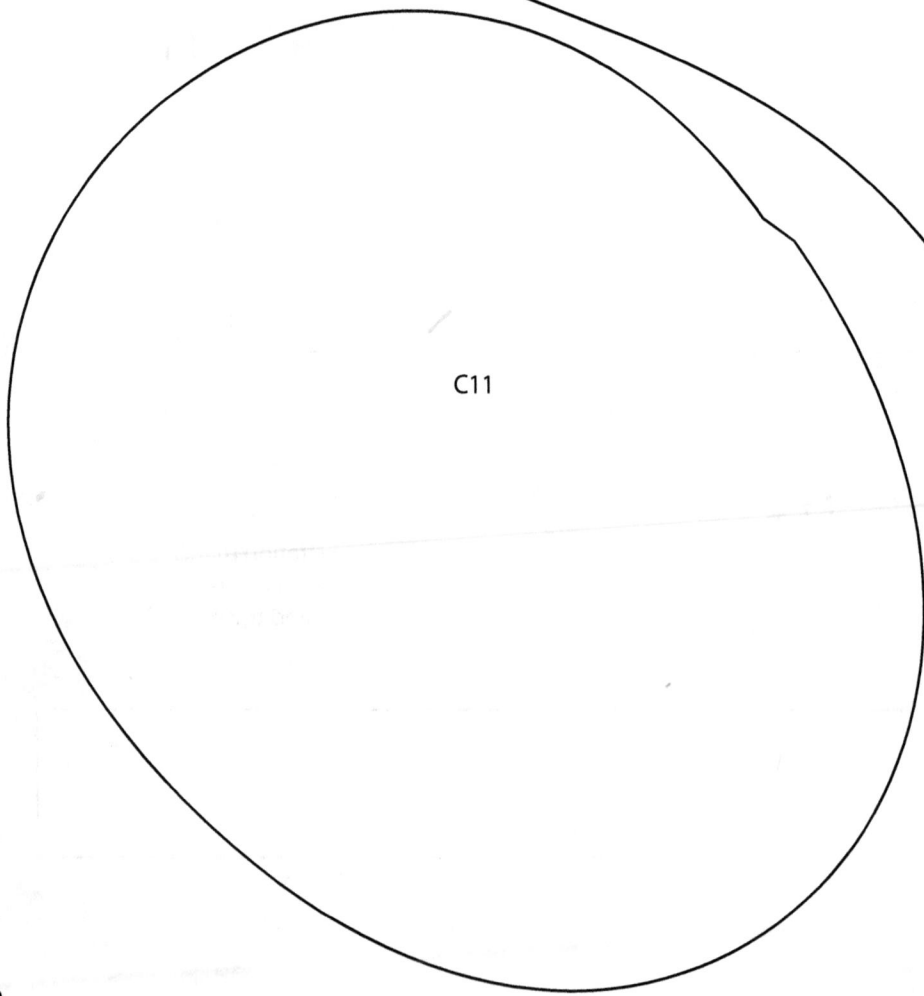

C11

Pattern reversed for tracing

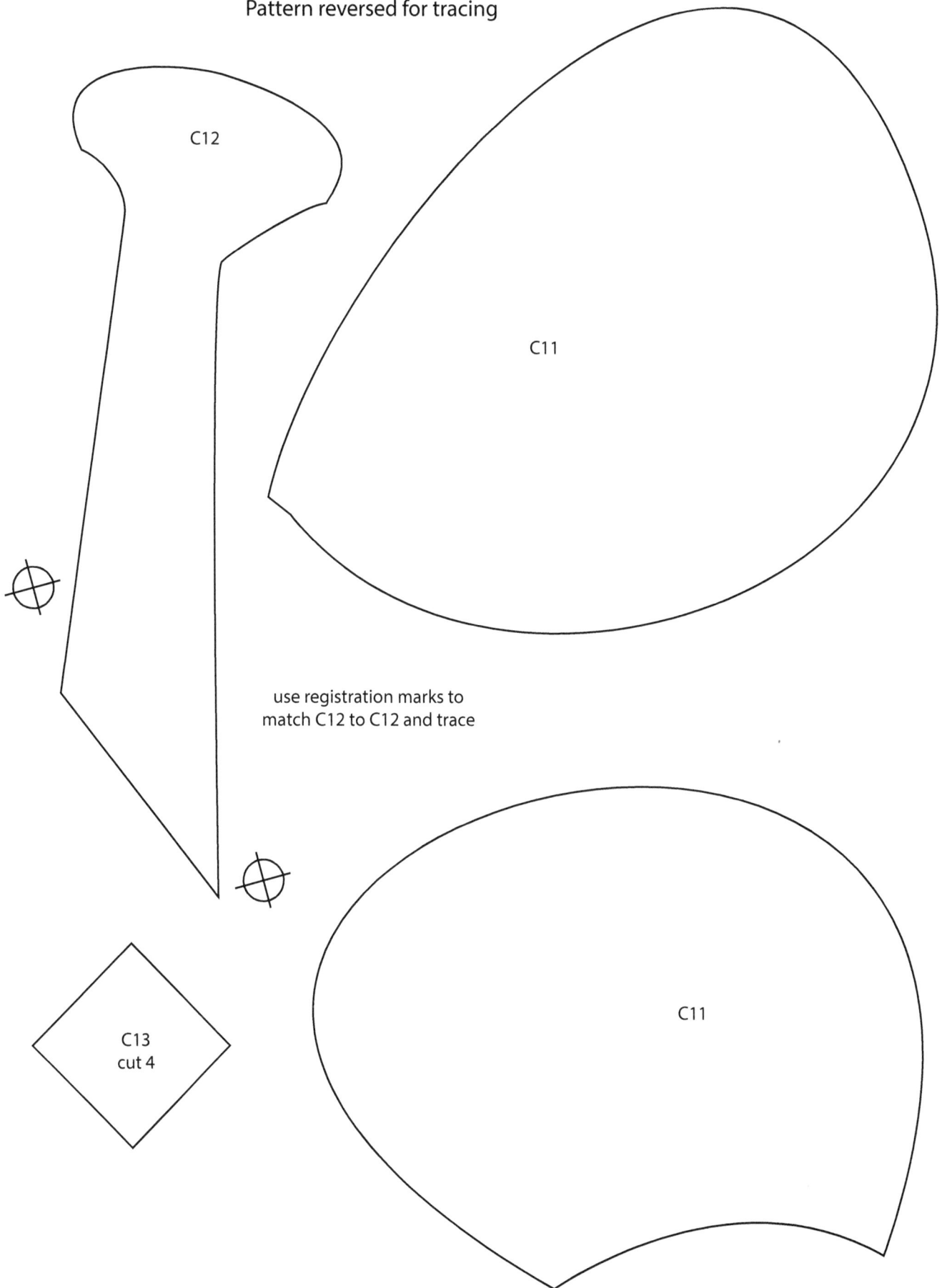

C12

C11

use registration marks to
match C12 to C12 and trace

C11

C13
cut 4

Pattern reversed for tracing

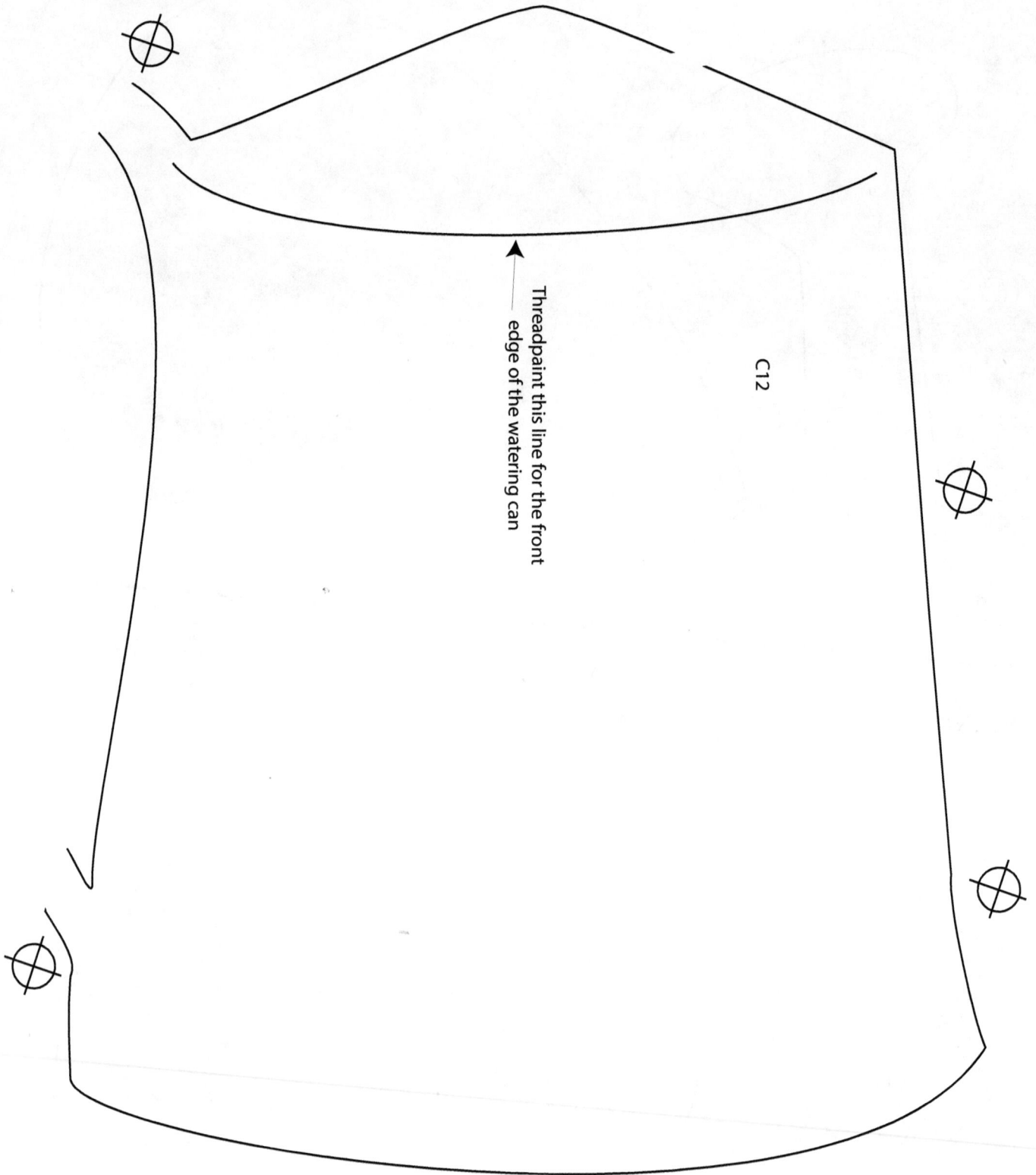

C12

Threadpaint this line for the front
edge of the watering can

Use registration marks
C12 handle to attach
to the watering can.

use registration marks to
match C12 to C12 and trace

Pattern reversed for tracing

use registration marks
to match C7 to C7 and trace
one this side and trace
one in reverse

use registration marks to
match C10 to C10
and trace

C7
cut 2
reverse 1

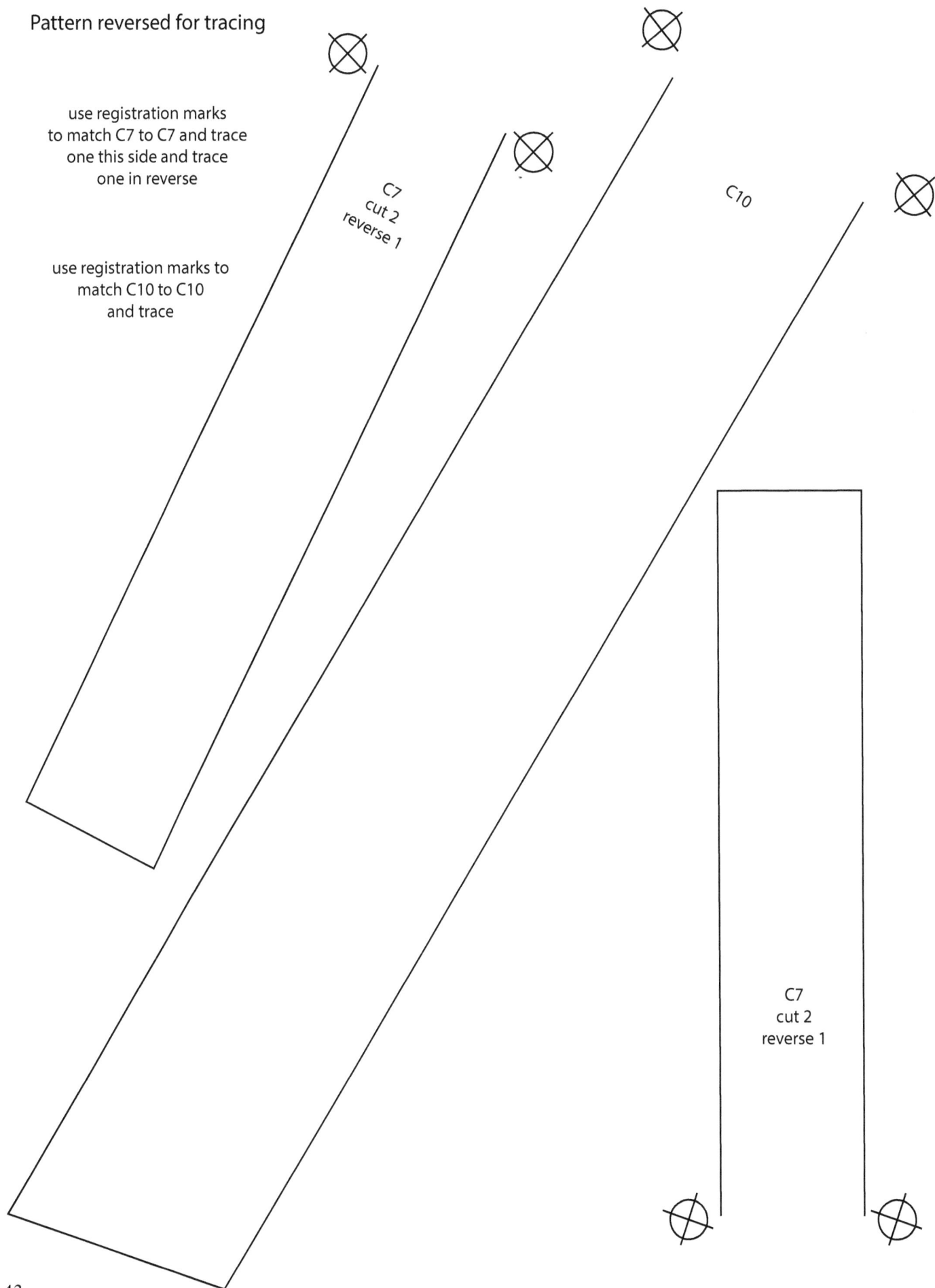

C10

C7
cut 2
reverse 1

Pattern reversed for tracing

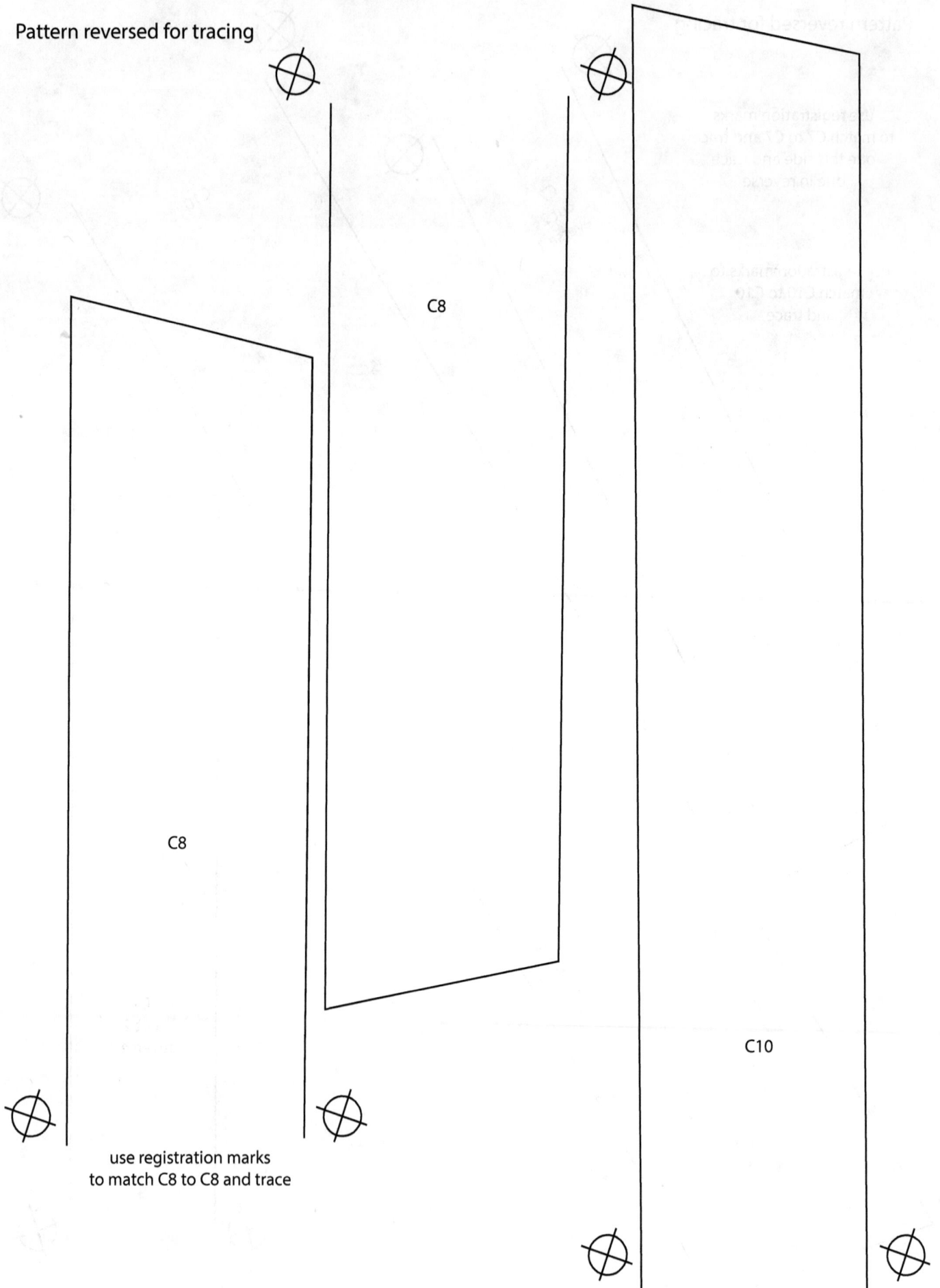

C8

C8

C8

C10

use registration marks
to match C8 to C8 and trace

Pattern reversed for tracing

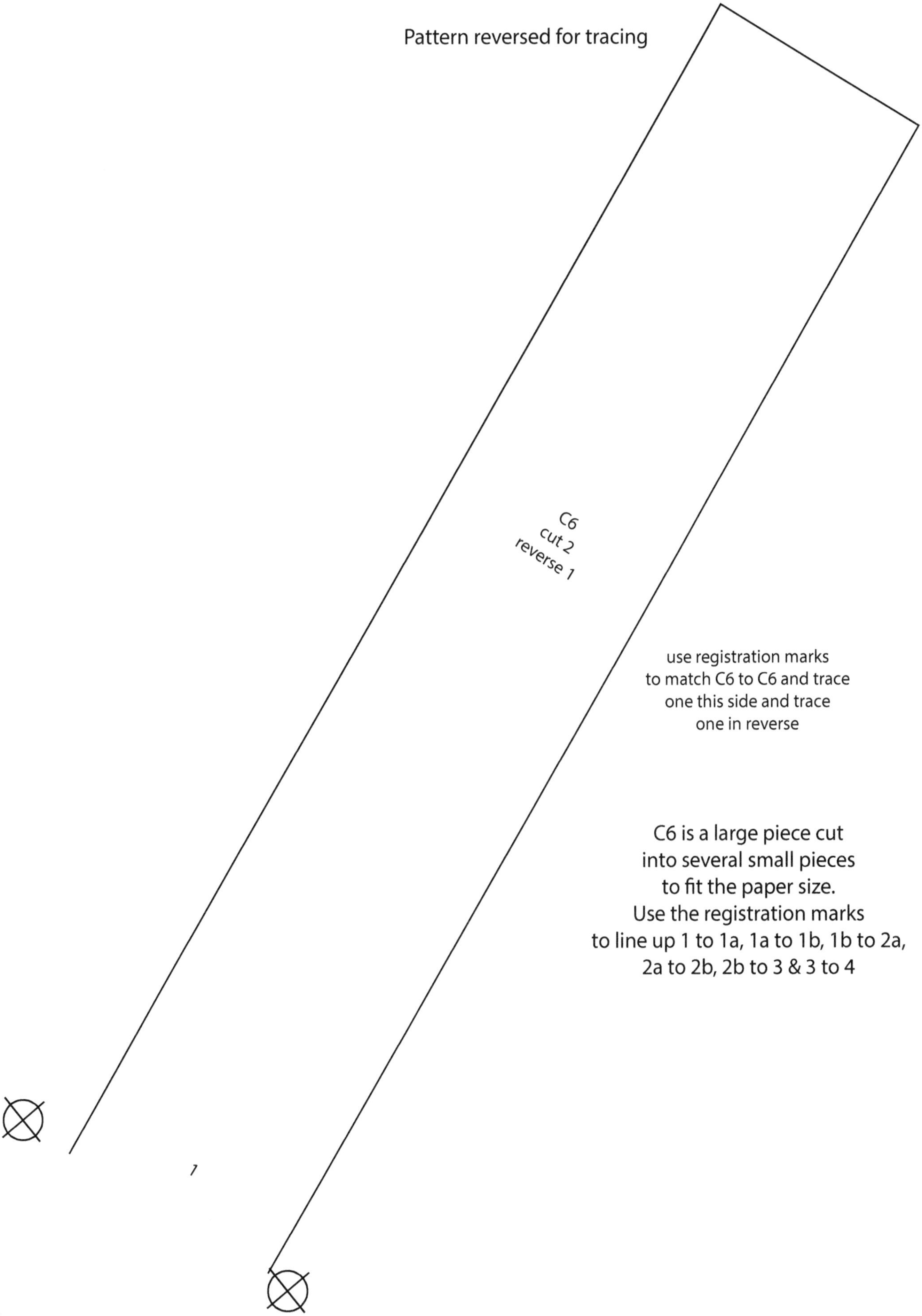

C6
cut 2
reverse 1

use registration marks
to match C6 to C6 and trace
one this side and trace
one in reverse

C6 is a large piece cut
into several small pieces
to fit the paper size.
Use the registration marks
to line up 1 to 1a, 1a to 1b, 1b to 2a,
2a to 2b, 2b to 3 & 3 to 4

1

C6 is a large piece cut
into several small pieces
to fit the paper size.
Use the registration marks
to line up 1 to 1a,
1a to 1b, 1b to 2a,
2a to 2b, 2b to 3 & 3 to 4

2a

C6
cut 2
reverse 1

2b

3

C6
cut 2
reverse 1

2b

use registration marks
to match C6 to C6 and trace
one this side and trace
one in reverse

3

4

Pattern reversed for tracing

use registration marks
to match C9 to C9 and trace
one this side and trace
one in reverse

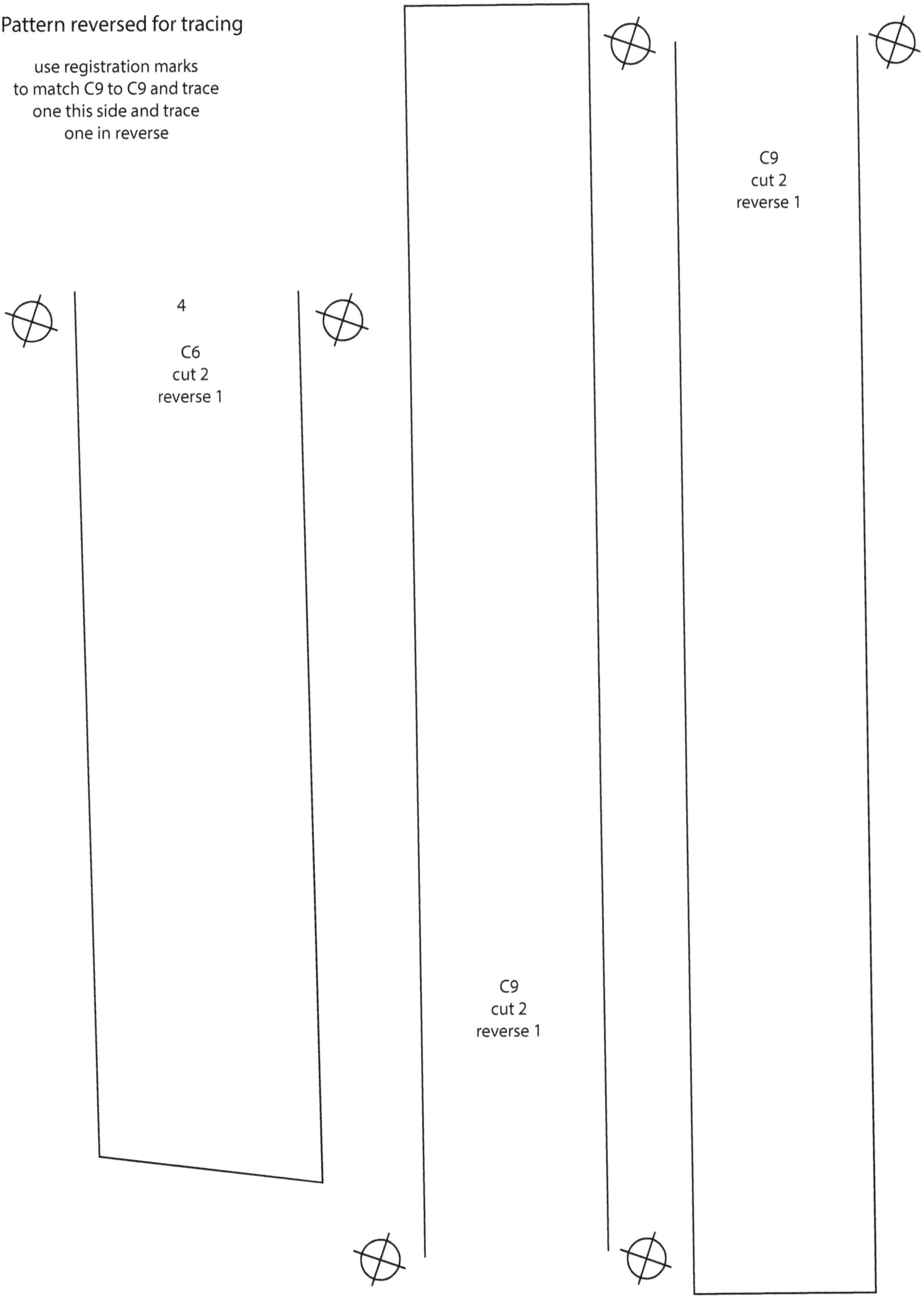

4

C6
cut 2
reverse 1

C9
cut 2
reverse 1

C9
cut 2
reverse 1

C9
cut 2
reverse 1

Pattern reversed for tracing

use registration marks to match vine 1
to vine 2 to vine 3
then trace

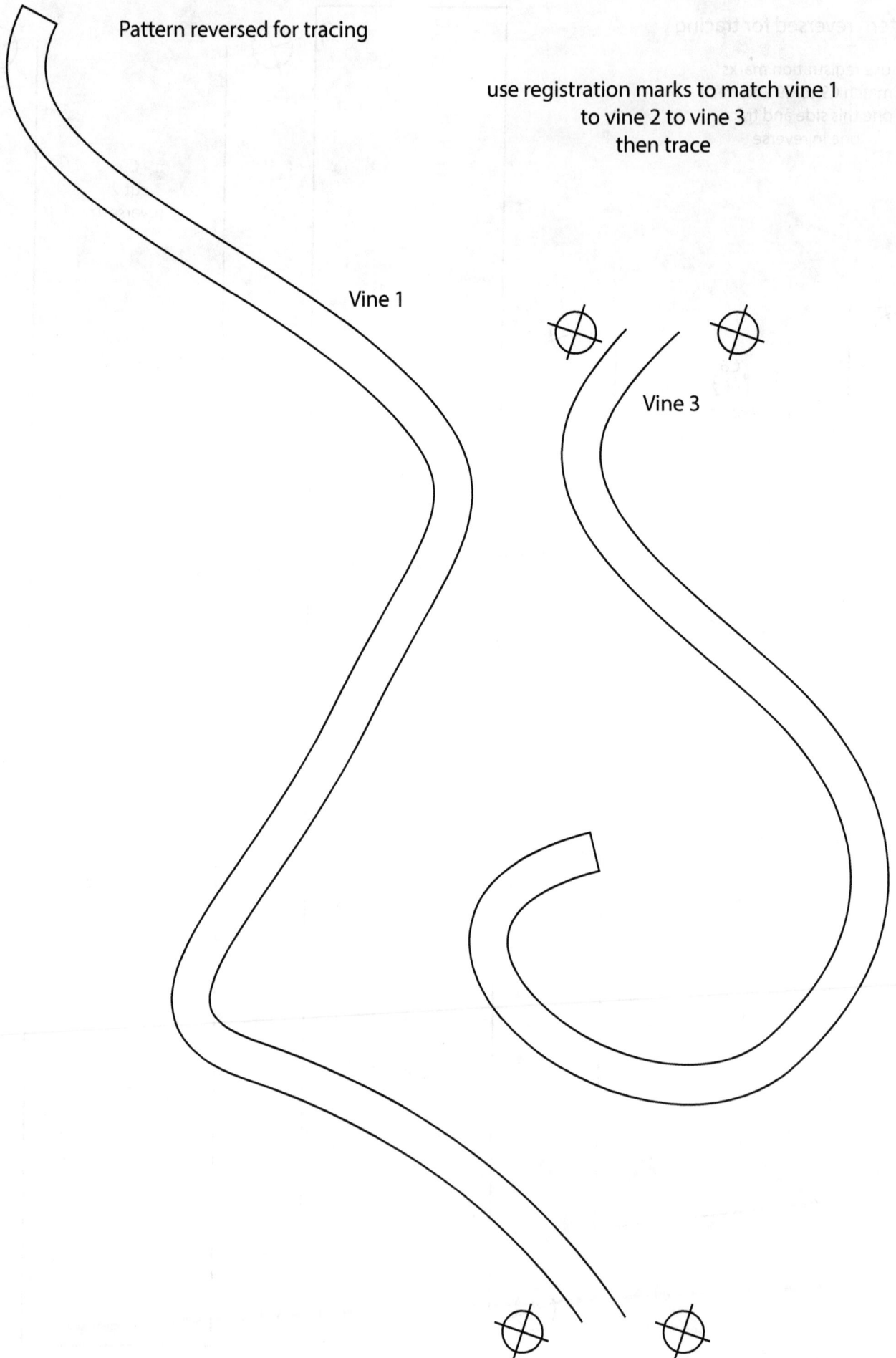

Vine 1

Vine 3

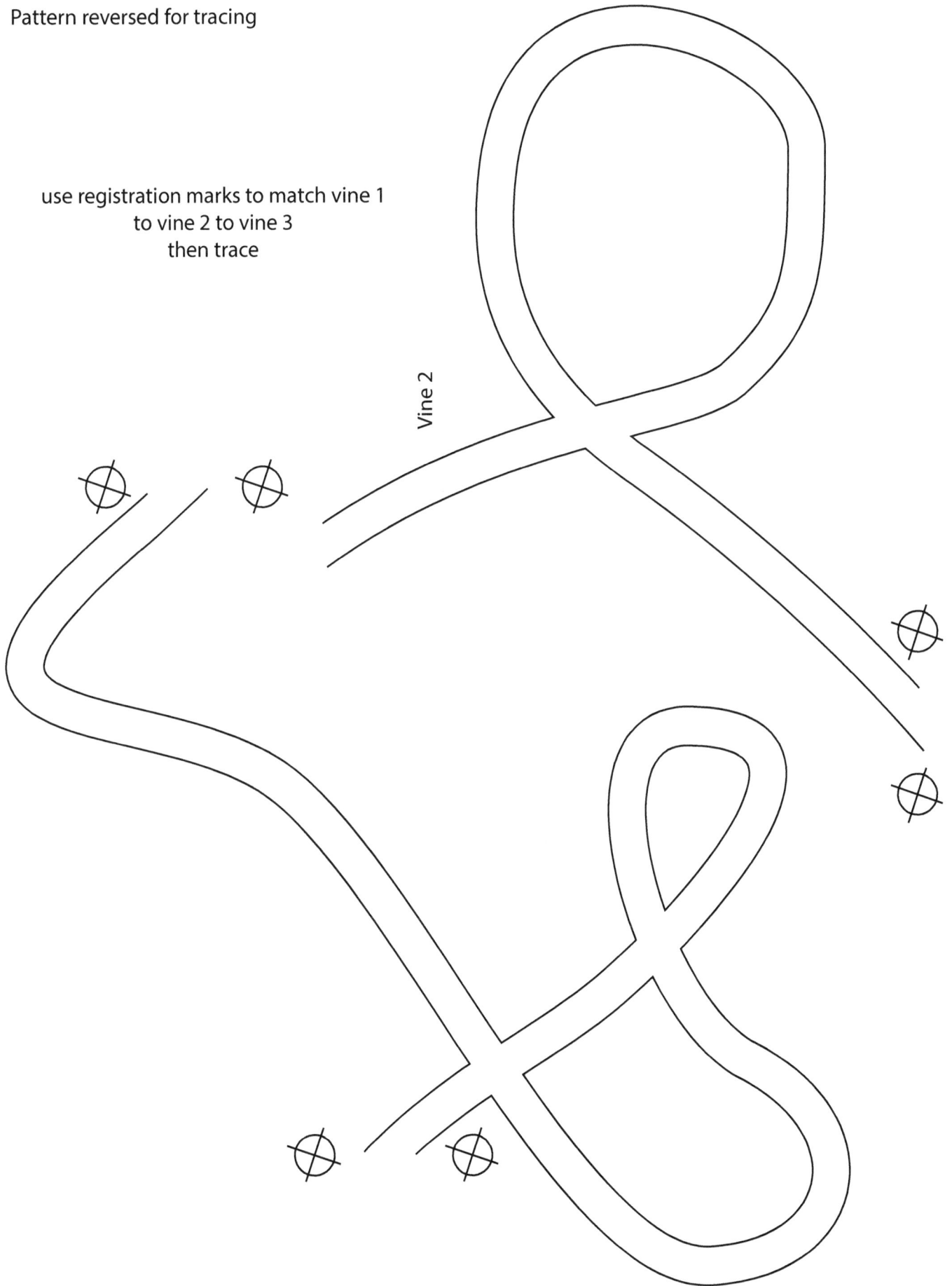

Pattern reversed for tracing

use registration marks to match vine 1
to vine 2 to vine 3
then trace

Vine 2

Pattern reversed for tracing

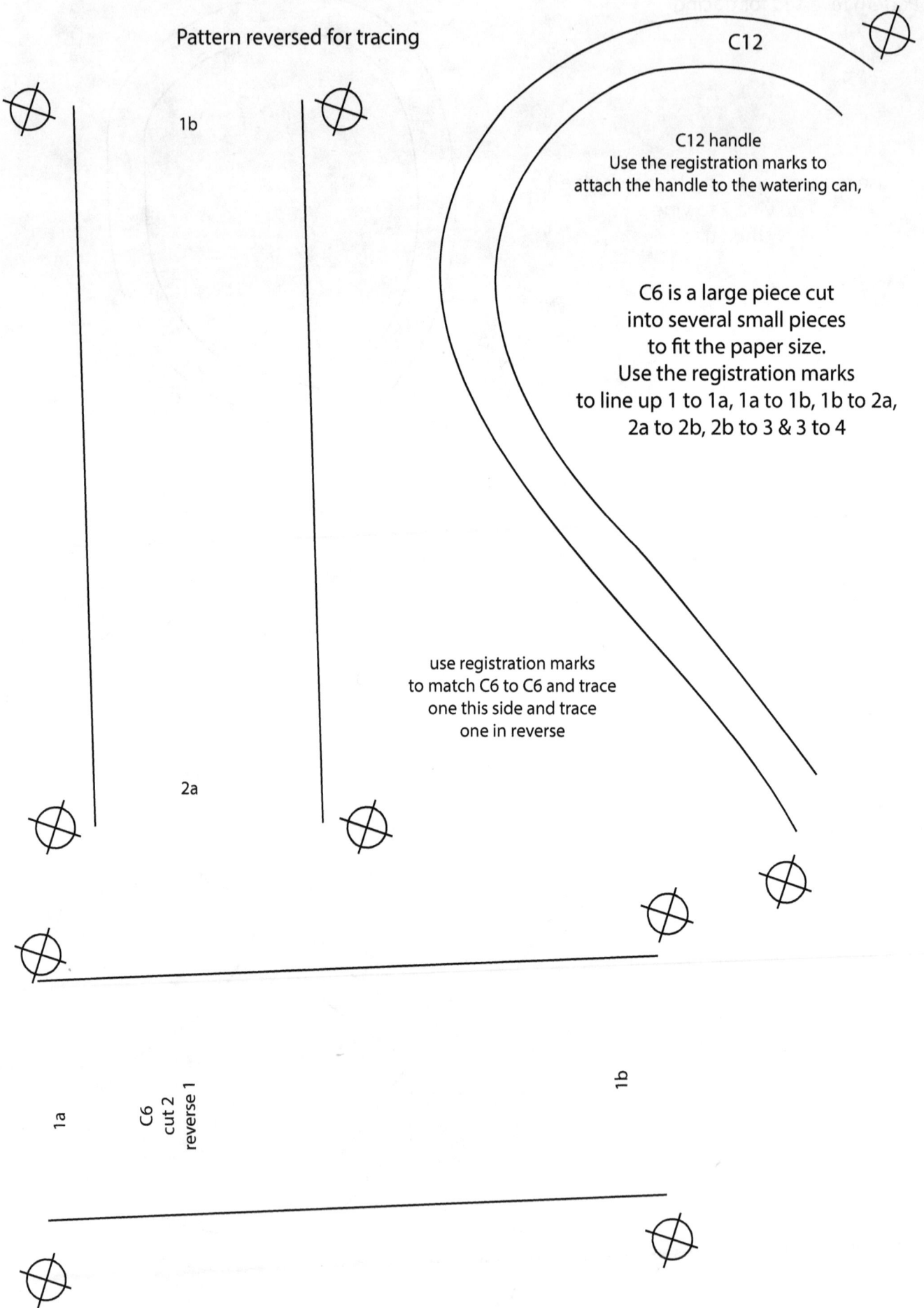

1b

C12

C12 handle
Use the registration marks to
attach the handle to the watering can,

C6 is a large piece cut
into several small pieces
to fit the paper size.
Use the registration marks
to line up 1 to 1a, 1a to 1b, 1b to 2a,
2a to 2b, 2b to 3 & 3 to 4

2a

use registration marks
to match C6 to C6 and trace
one this side and trace
one in reverse

1a

C6
cut 2
reverse 1

1b

the story behind the quilt block

As with the other blocks in this quilt, this one has a definite significance to me.

The composition of this block is a familiar one to me. As I sit in my studio on the second floor of the home my husband and I have built, I see this view every day.

The windmill, a flagpole proudly flying the Texas flag, and this birdhouse stand very close to one another in an area reserved to welcome guests.

We sometimes hang a hummingbird feeder from the pole, but this day one of my husband's birdhouse designs gives sanctuary to flying guests. He has designed and placed birdhouses throughout the interior fencing of our property. Remember those cows?

I don't consider myself THAT old, but my paternal grandfather came to the prairie in a covered wagon! He was a baby, but he made the trip in a wagon. This was not some great, great, great grandfather, no! It was my father's father!

The wagon wheel in this block stands as a reminder of my roots, and all those braving the terrain for a new life filled with scenic beauty and prosperity.

Beyond the Gate

Beyond the Gate

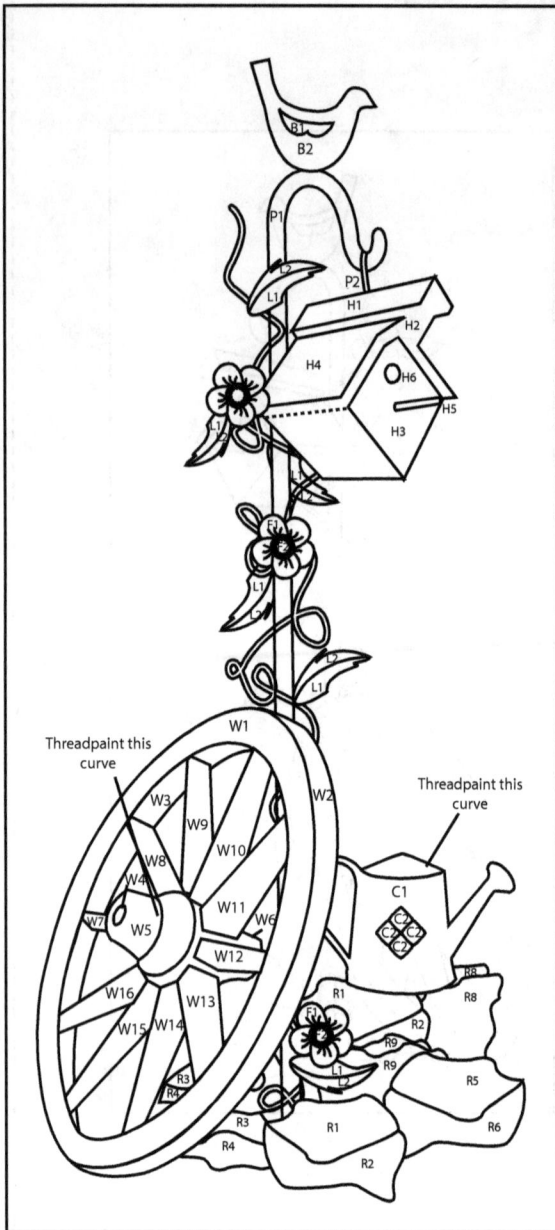

Threadpaint this curve

Threadpaint this curve

Fabric Requirements:

Block:
34" x 72 ½" purple

Applique:

flowers (3)	17" x 8"
flower centers (3)	4" x 4"
light leaves	13" x 8"
medium leaves	13" x 8"
vines (2) fabric or ¼" fusible bias tape	12" x 31"
birdhouse pole	8" x 60"
wagon wheel	16" x 30"
wagon wheel inside/outside edges (2)	16" x 30"
spokes	18" x 26"
watering can	15" x 10"
watering can 4 square	3" x 3" ea.
bird	9" x 7"
bird wing	4" x 3"
rocks, light	24" x 17"
rocks, shadow	16" x 12"
front axel	7" x 6"
rear axel	7" x 8"
birdhouse roof [H1 & [H4]	10" x 12"
birdhouse front [H3]	12" x 6"
birdhouse frame [H2]	15" x 13"
remaining birdhouse pieces	8" x 8"

Paper backed web (17"):
4 yards

Stabilizer:
To prevent fabric puckering, use your favorite type of stabilizer behind the appliqué pieces. Tear away stabilizer is a good choice for this purpose.

Thread:
Matching or contrasting thread, as you prefer.

Suggestion:
Use two different colors for the flower petals, one lighter than the other. Embellish the flower with embroidery thread.

For added emphasis, put long running stitches within each of the blocks.

Beyond the Gate

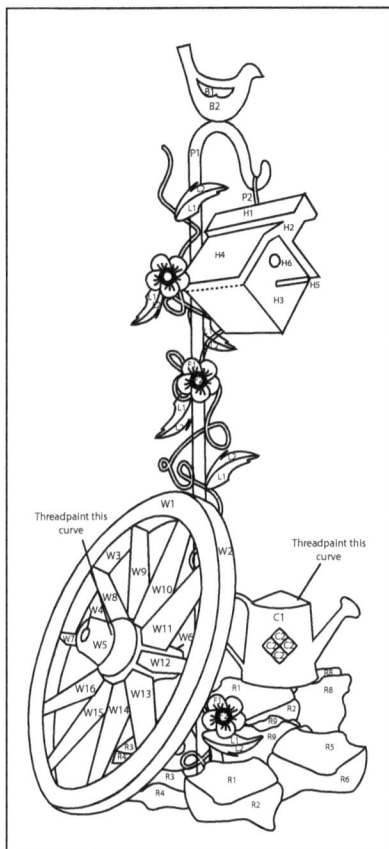

Rotary Cutting
- Cut [1] background rectangle 34" x 72 ½"
  OR cut [2] 34" x 36 ½", sew together along 36½" edge

- Trace applique pieces on the paper backed web material
- Press paper backed web to the wrong side of the applique fabric
- Cut out applique pieces

On a teflon or applique sheet:
- **Birdhouse Unit** (for closer view see positioning diagram)
  - Place [H1] behind [H2], place [H5] behind [H3]
  - Place [H9] over [H8], place [H4] behind [H3]
  - Place [H6] & [H7] on [H8]
  - Press
- **Wagon Wheel Unit - do not press until all pieces are set**
        (for closer view see positioning diagram)
  - Place rims [W3] and [W2] behind [W1]
  - Place axle [W5] over [W6]
  - Place spokes [W7] thru [W16]
  - Place [W4] over [W5]
  - Press
- **Flower Unit** (same instructions as for month 1, smaller size)
  - Create a flower unit by overlapping [5] petals [F1] in a circular shape
  - Place the center circle [F2] over the petals
  - Press
  - Repeat the process for [4] more petals
- **Leaf Unit** (same instructions as for month 1, smaller size)
  - Create a leaf unit by overlapping the light/dark pieces
  - Press
  - Repeat the process for [4] more petals
- **Rocks Unit** (for closer view see positioning diagram)
  - Place rock pieces [R1] over [R2], press, place [R3] over [R4], press
  - Place [R5] over [R6], press, place [R8] over [R8], press
  - Don't group them together & press until placed on background
- **Watering Can Unit** (for closer view see positioning diagram)
  - Place [4] square pieces [C13] on point on the watering can [C12]
  - Press

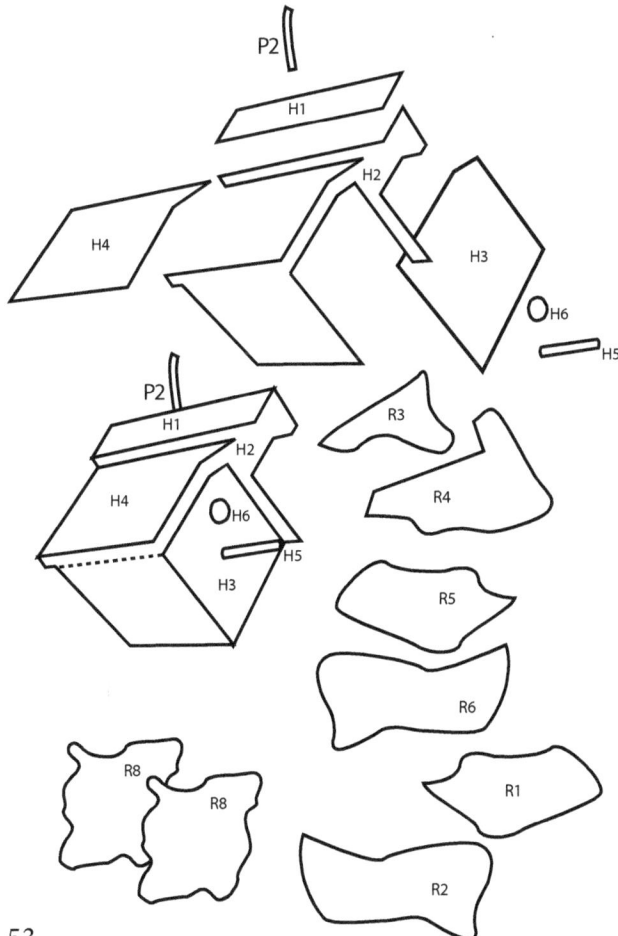

Complete the block
- Place birdhouse holder on background
- Place bird on top of the holder
- Place birdhouse unit on holder by using [P2]
- Place rocks around base of holder
- Place watering can unit on rocks
- Place vine on birdhouse holder
- Place flowers/leaf units over vine
- Press wagon wheel to lean on birdhouse holder
- When all pieces are positioned, press

Applique
- Use a tear away stabilizer behind each block and applique the edges using a blanket stitch, satin stitch, or close zig zag stitch
- Threadpaint watering can top and axle piece

Beyond the Gate

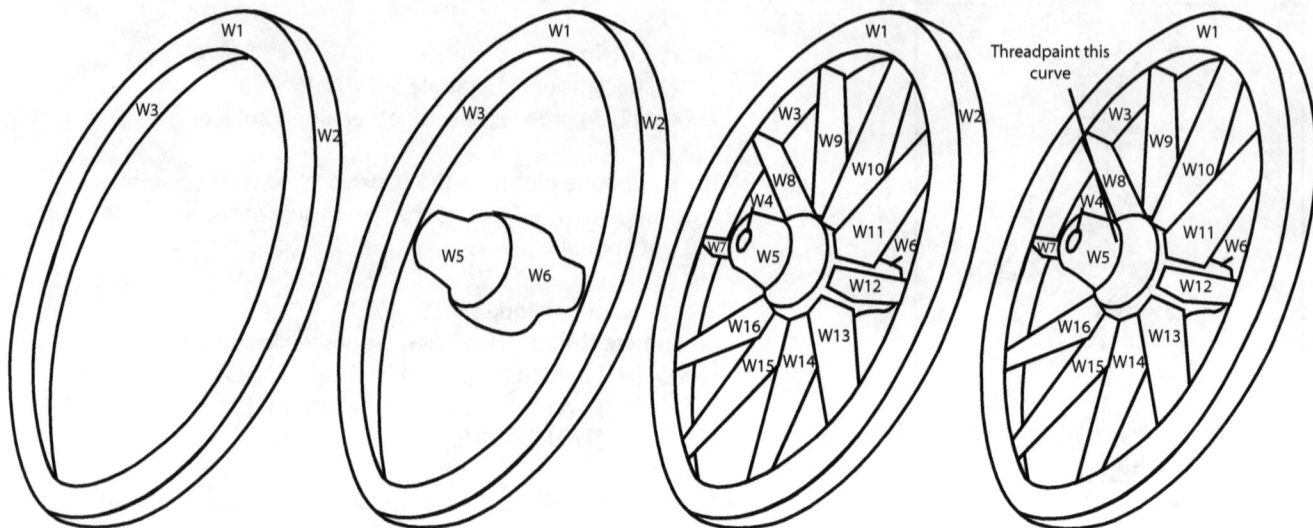

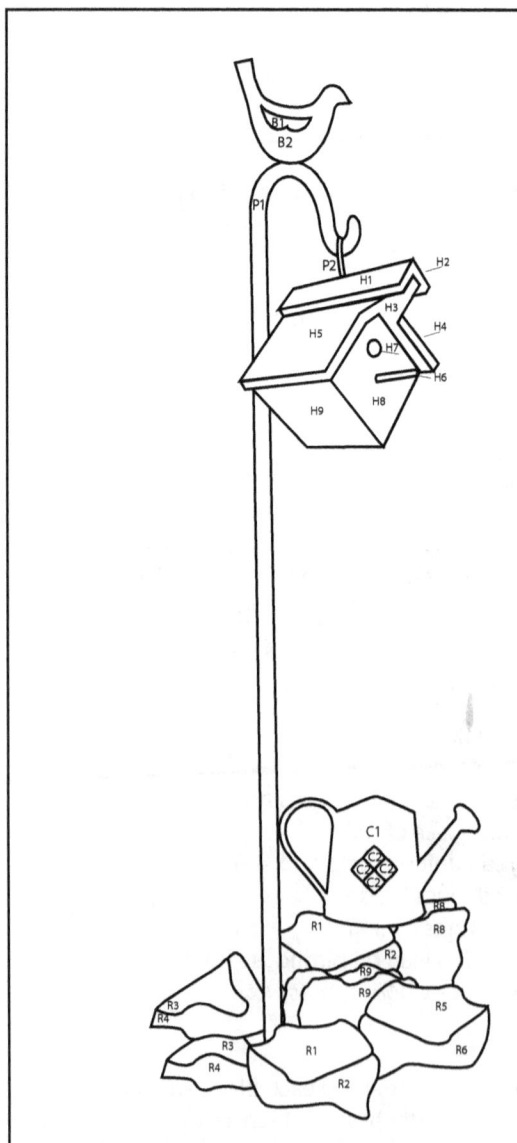

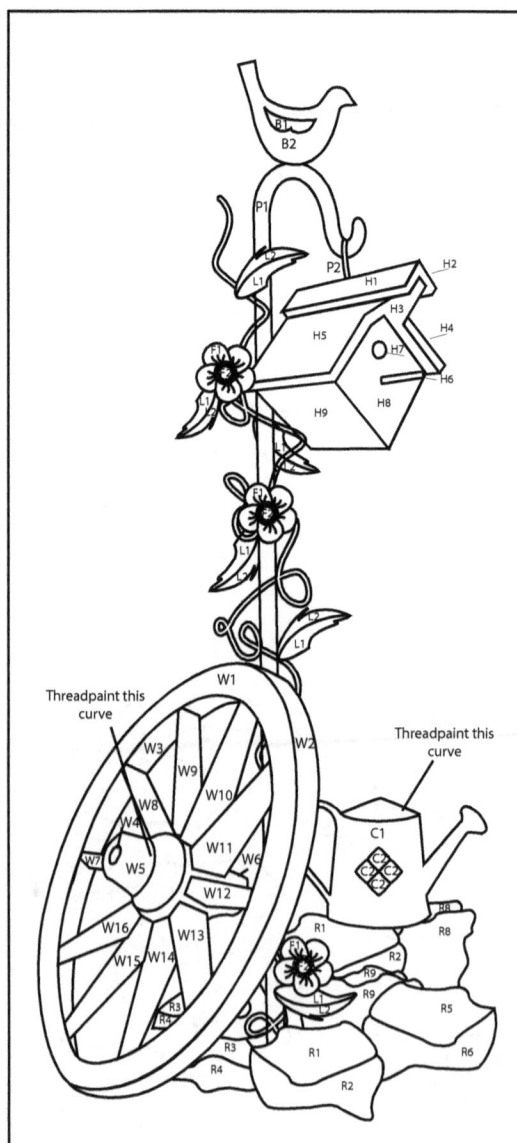

W1
W3
W2

W1
W3
W2
W5
W6

W1
Threadpaint this curve
W3
W9
W8
W10
W4
W7
W5
W11
W6
W12
W16
W13
W15 W14

W1
W3
W9
W8
W10
W4
W7
W5
W11
W6
W12
W16
W13
W15 W14

B1
B2
P1
P2
H1
H2
H3
H4
H5
H7
H6
H8
H9
C1
C2
R1
R8
R9
R2
R3
R9
R4
R3
R1
R5
R2
R6

B1
B2
P1
L1
P2
L1
H1
H2
H3
H4
H5
H7
H6
H8
L1
L1
Threadpaint this curve
W1
W3
W2
W9
W8
W10
W4
W11
W6
W7
W5
W12
W16
W13
W15 W14
Threadpaint this curve
C1
C2
R1
R8
R9
R2
L1
R3
R9
R4
R3
R1
R5
R2
R6

Positioning Diagram

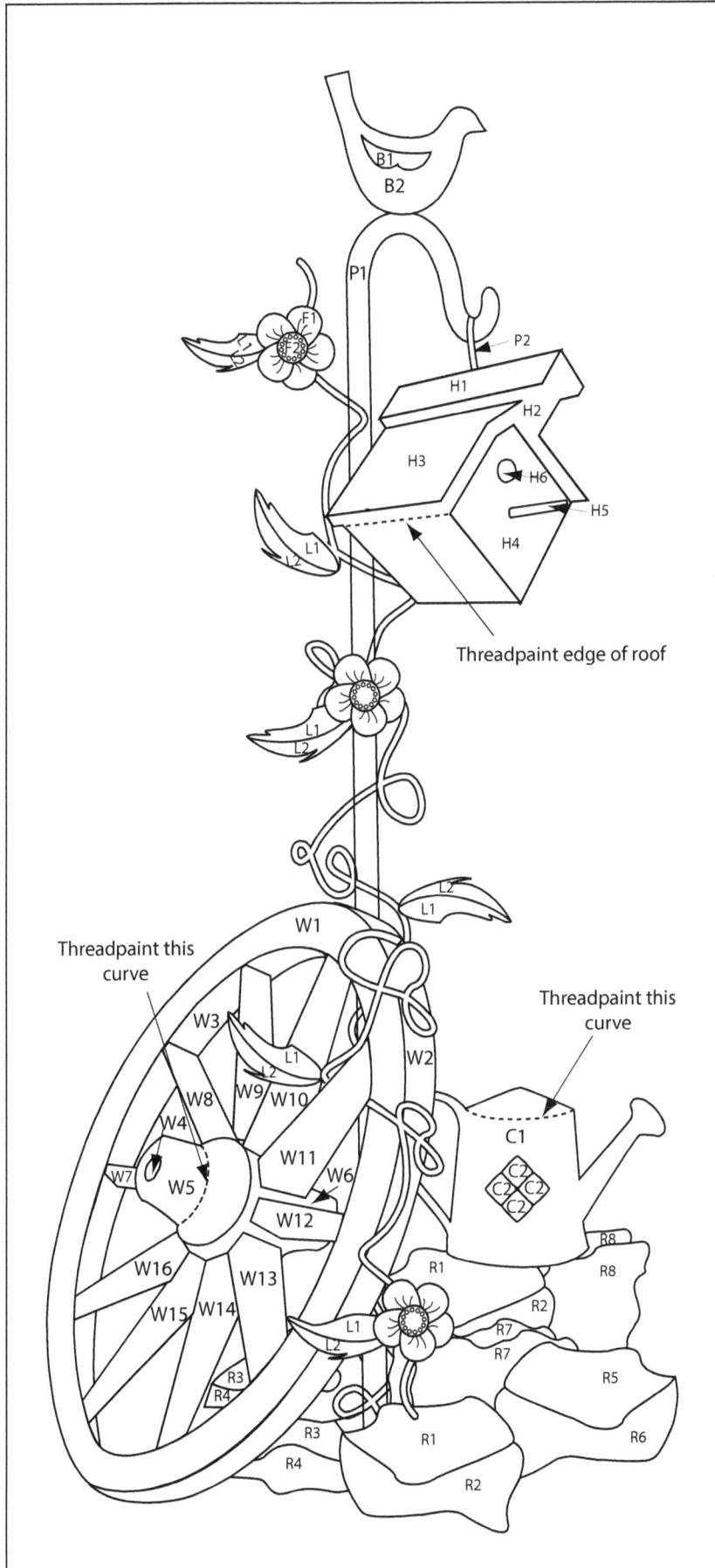

Threadpaint edge of roof

Threadpaint this curve

Threadpaint this curve

Place vines, flowers, and rocks at your discretion.

H6

Reversed for tracing

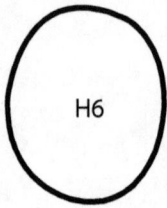

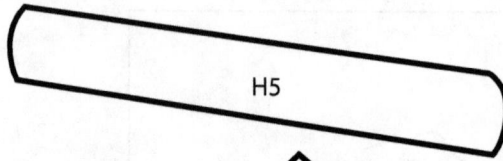

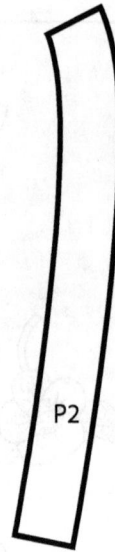

H5

bird house
hanger

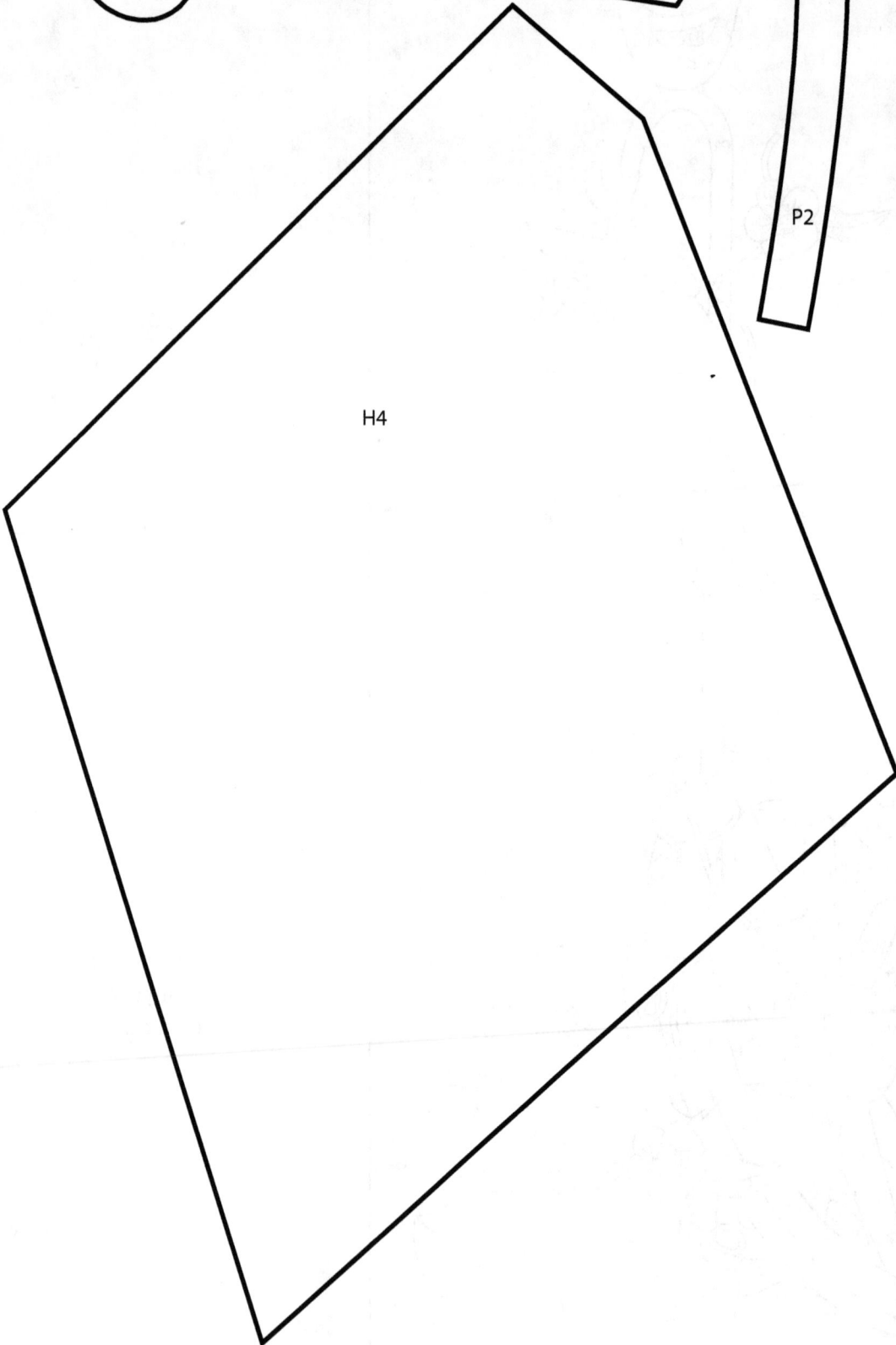

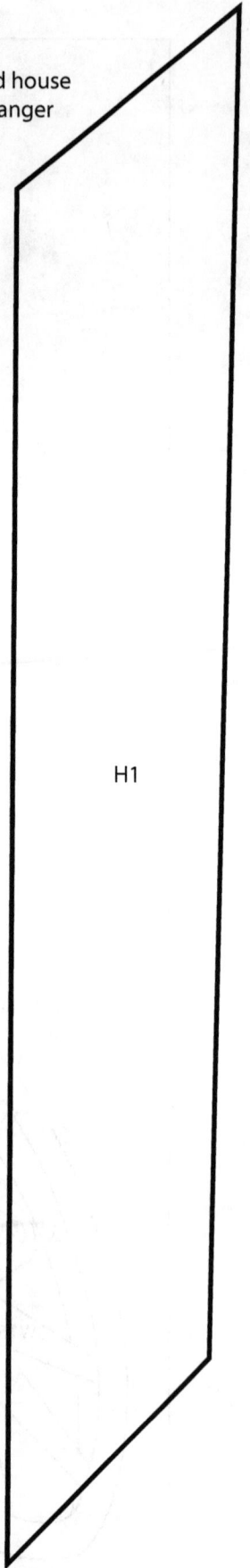

P2

H4

H1

56

Reversed for tracing

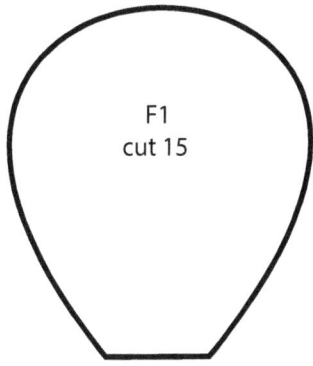

F1
cut 15

H3

H3

match registration marks
to form H3

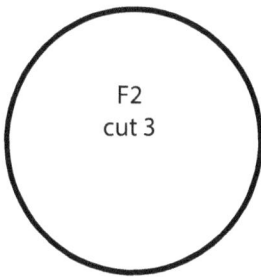

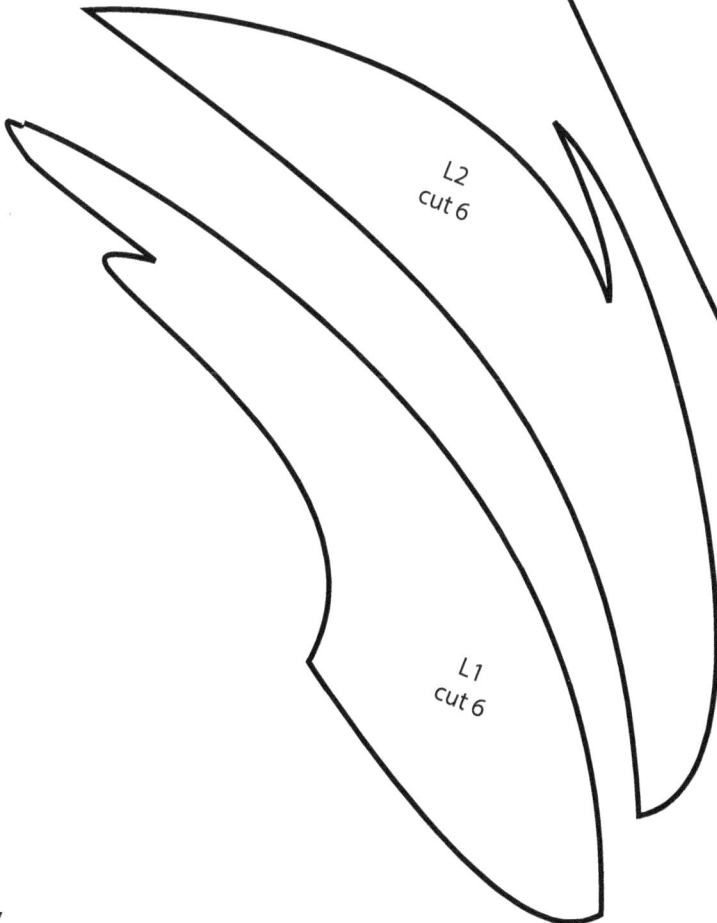

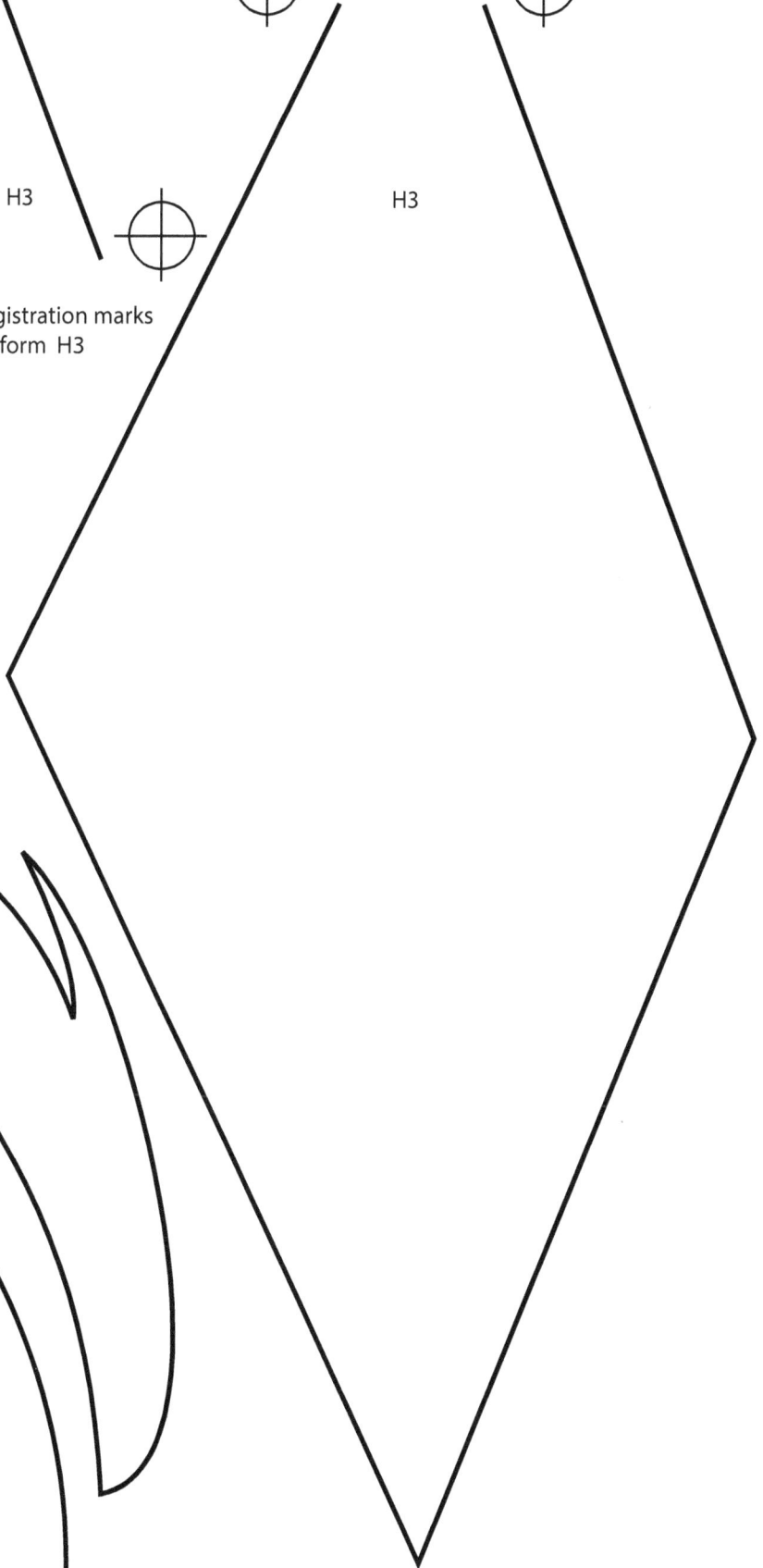

F2
cut 3

L2
cut 6

L1
cut 6

Reversed for tracing

match registration marks
to form H2
(2 parts to form 1 H2 pattern piece)

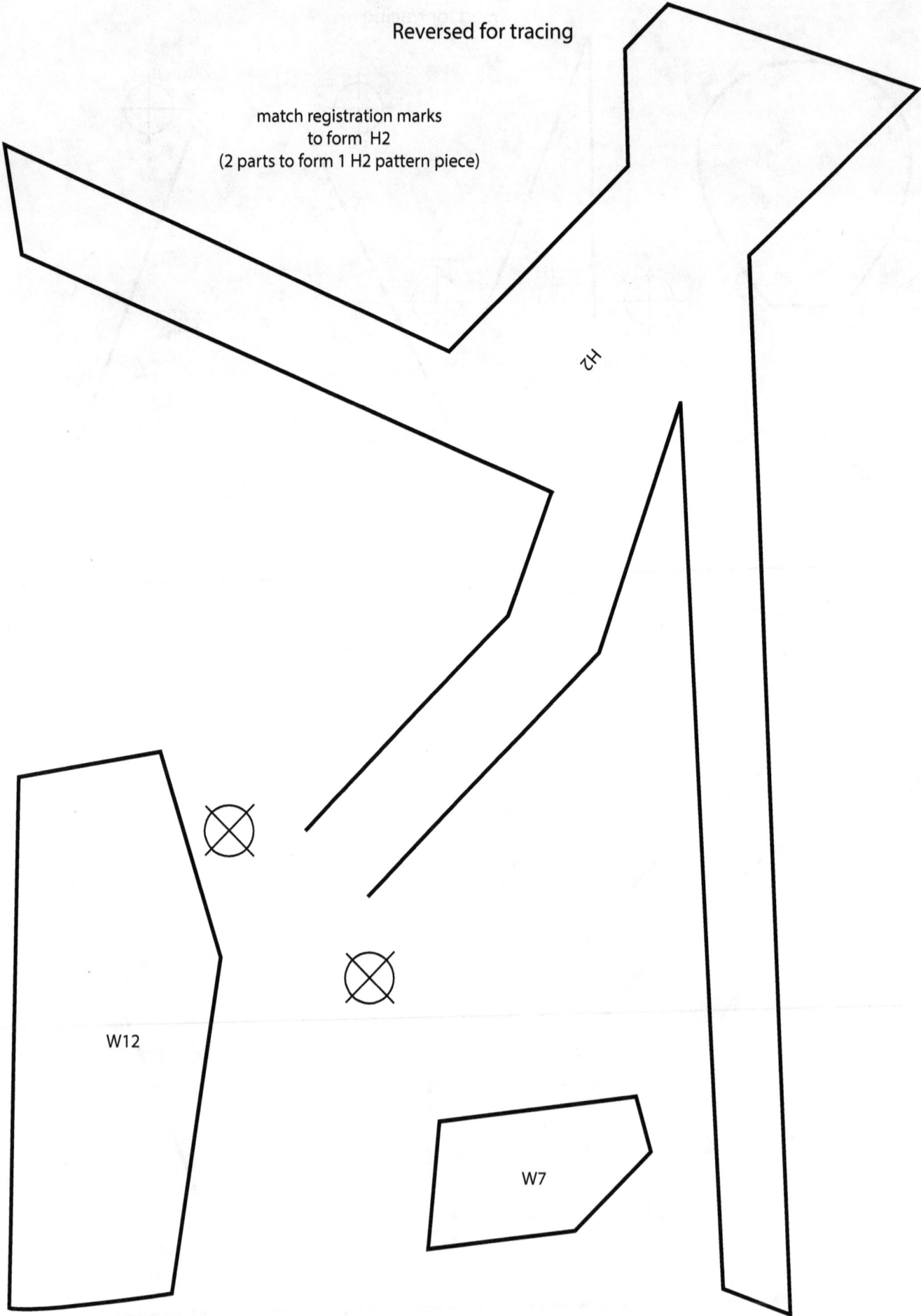

H2

W12

W7

Reversed for tracing

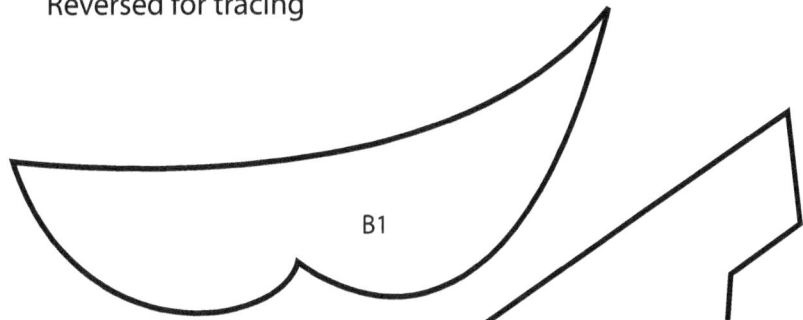

B1

match registration marks
to form H2
(2 parts to form 1 H2 pattern piece)

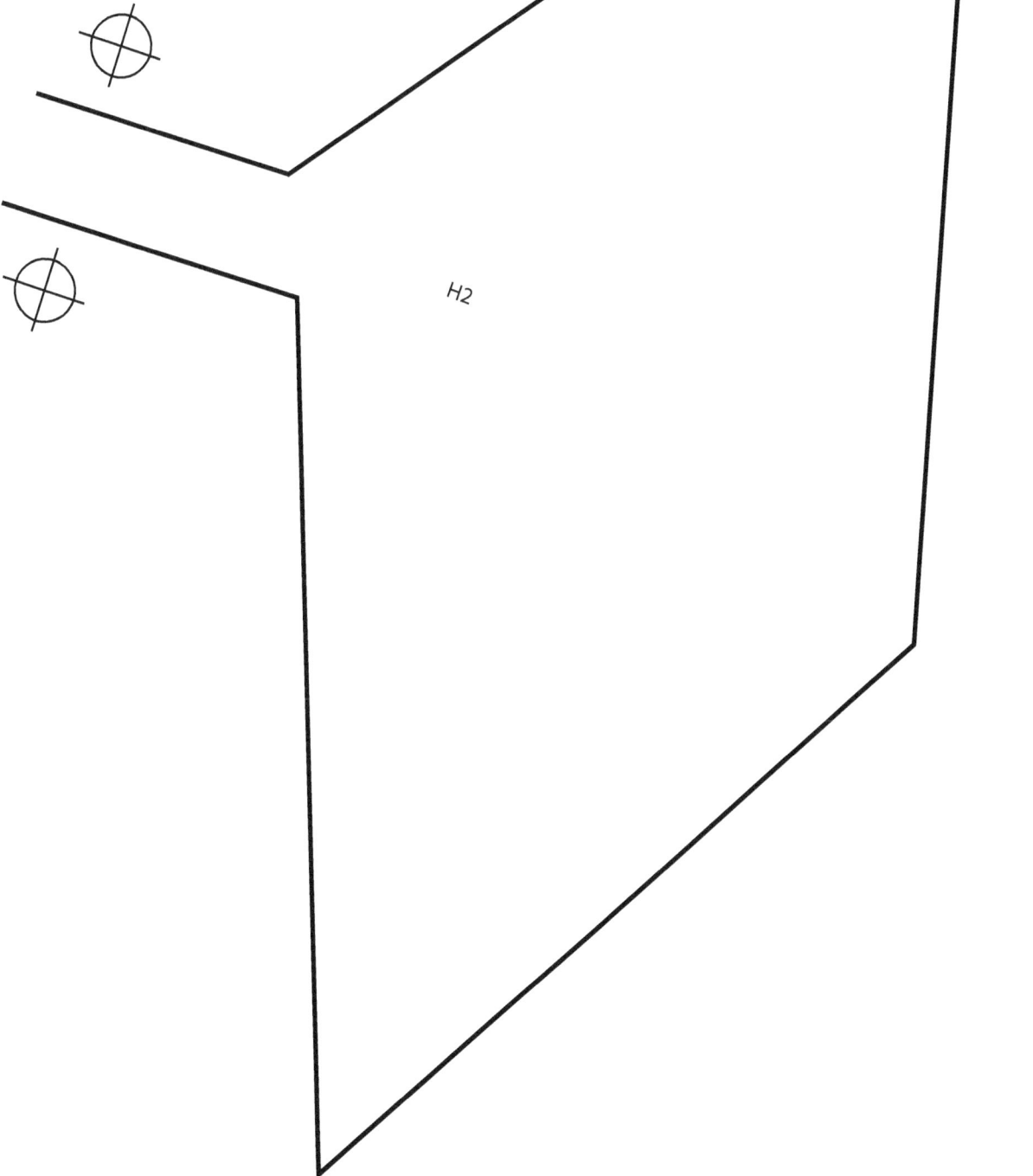

H2

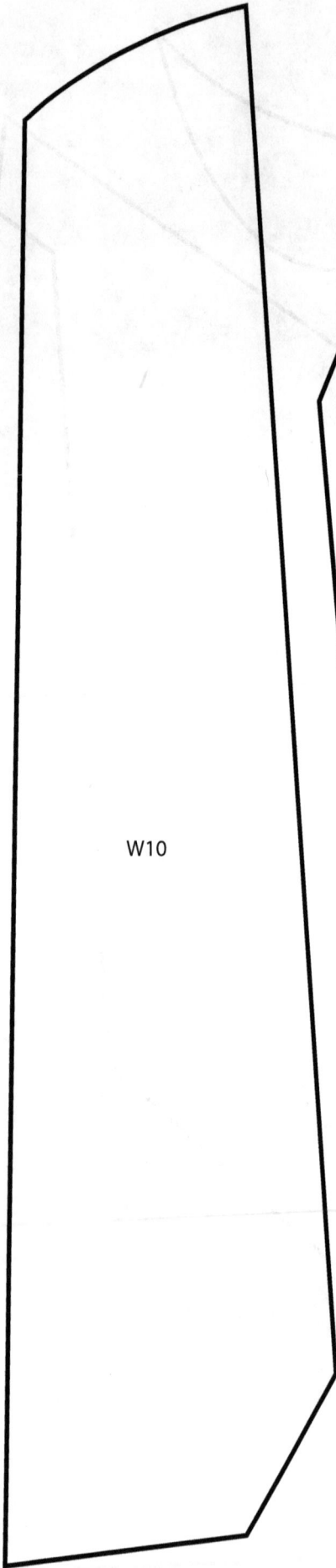

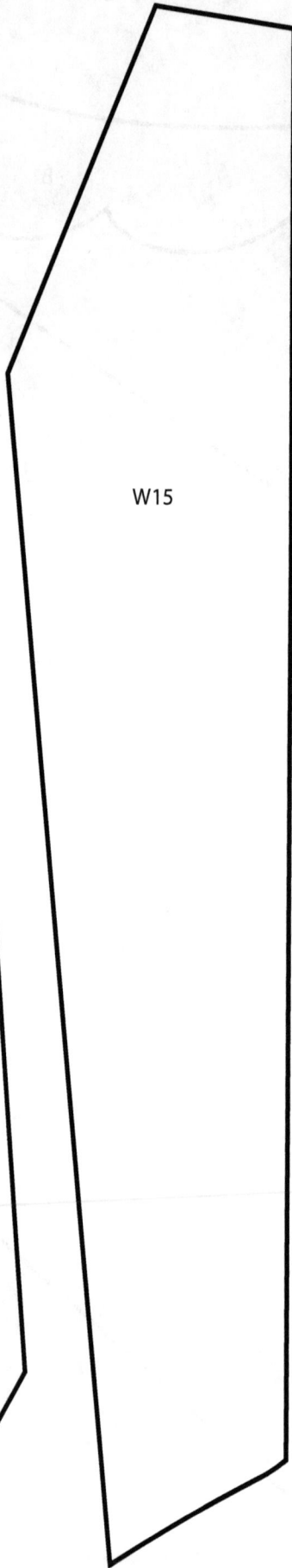

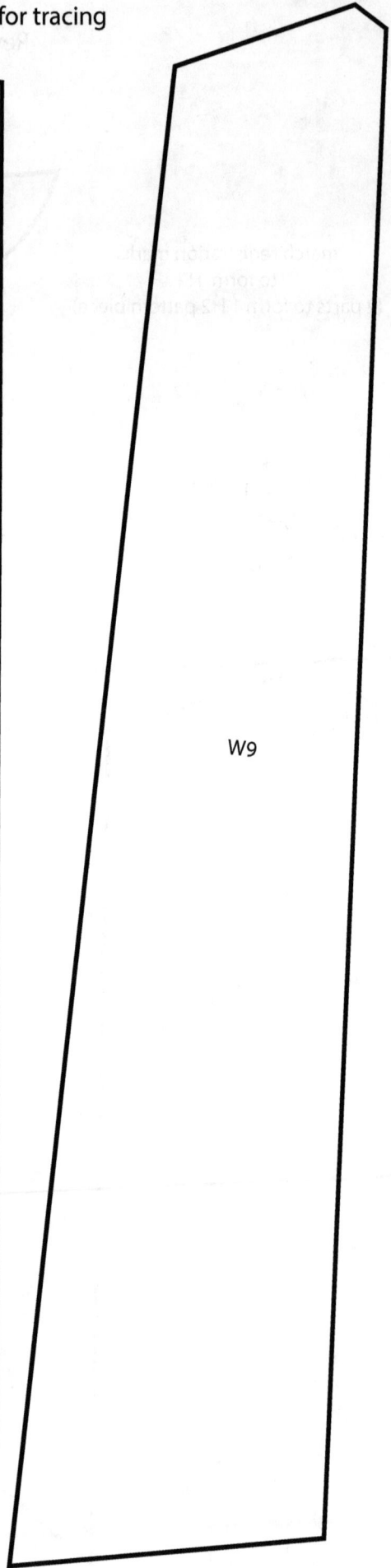

W15

W9

W10

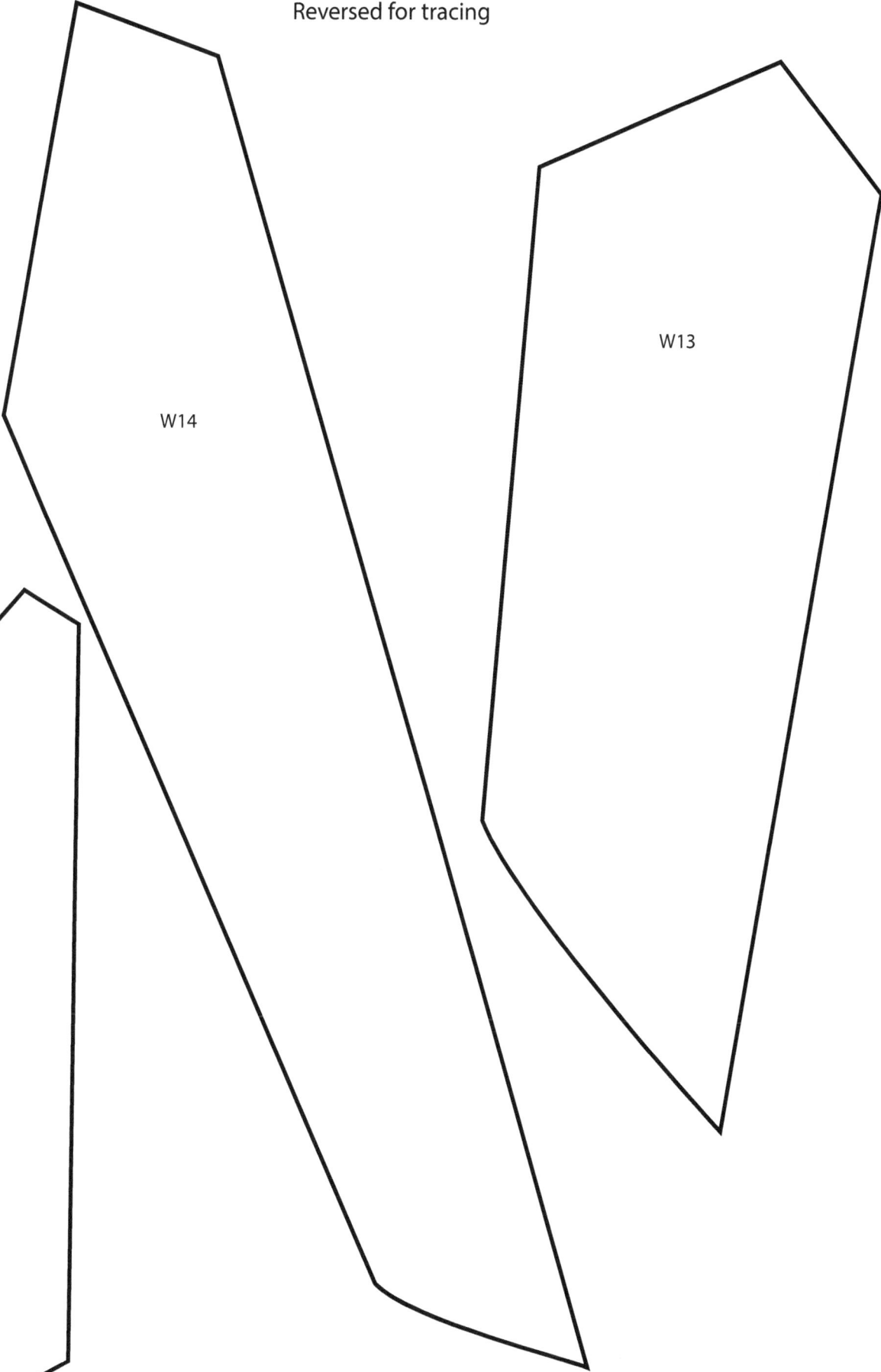

W14

W13

W8

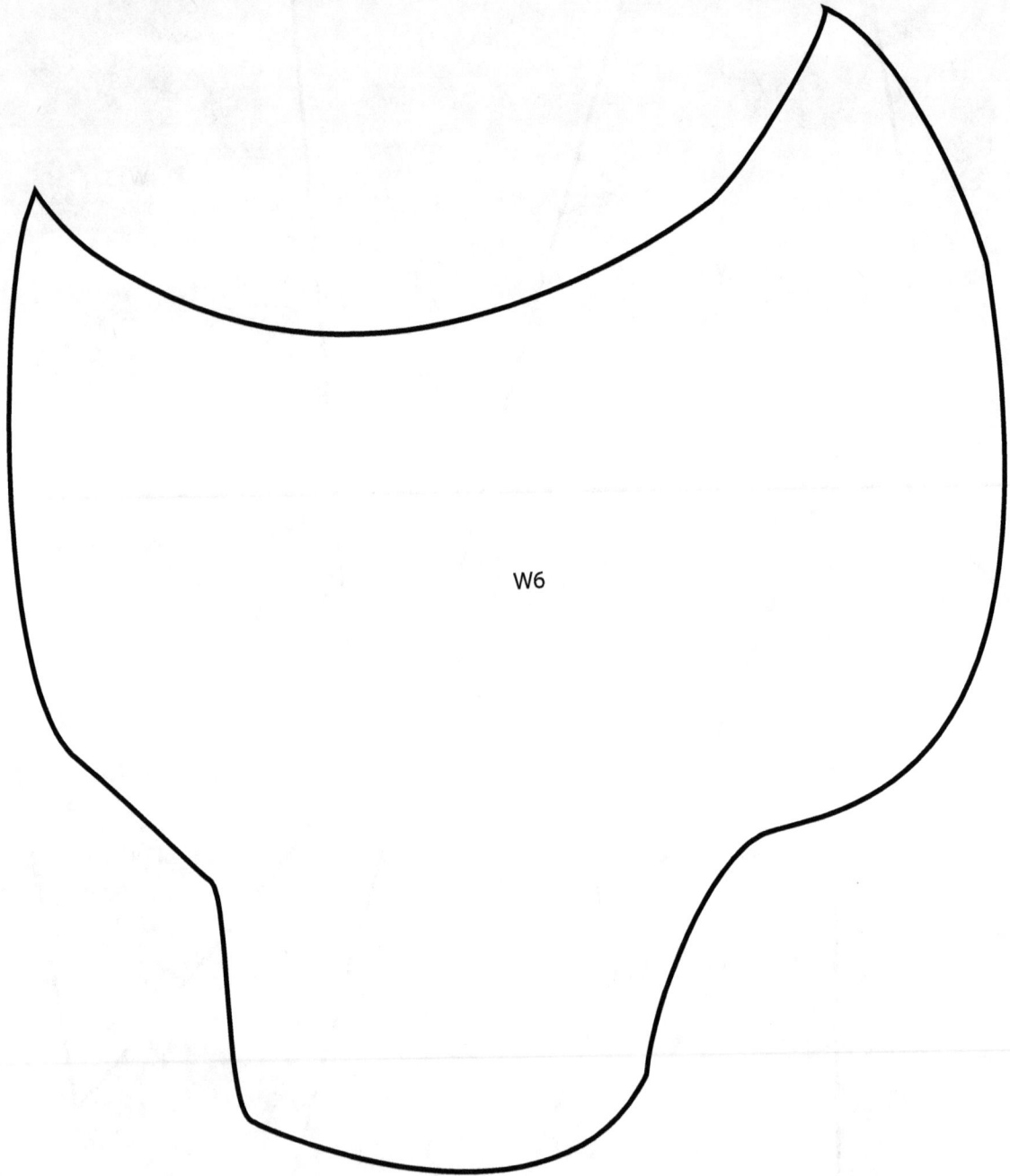

W6

R1
cut 2

R2
cut 2

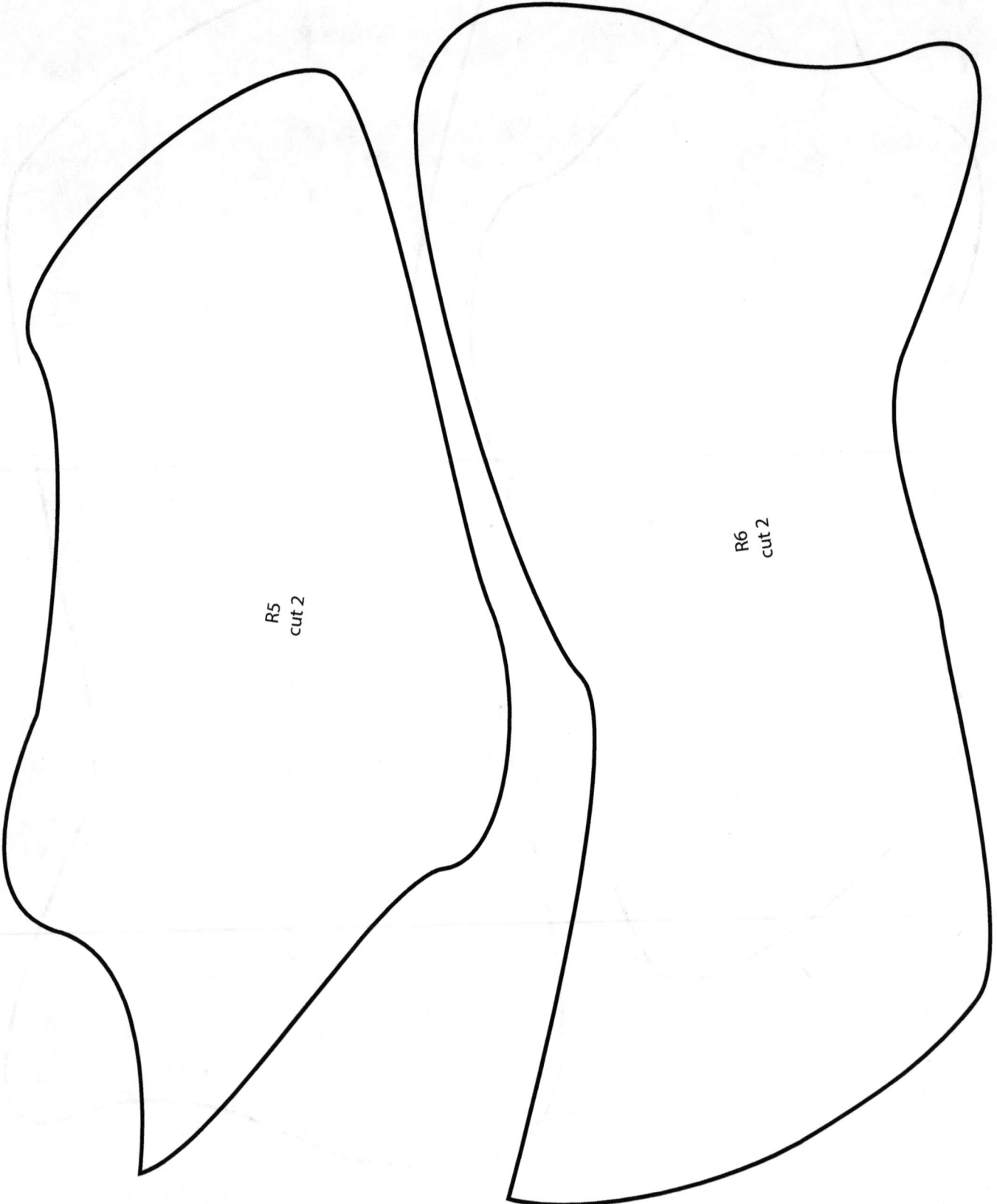

R5
cut 2

R6
cut 2

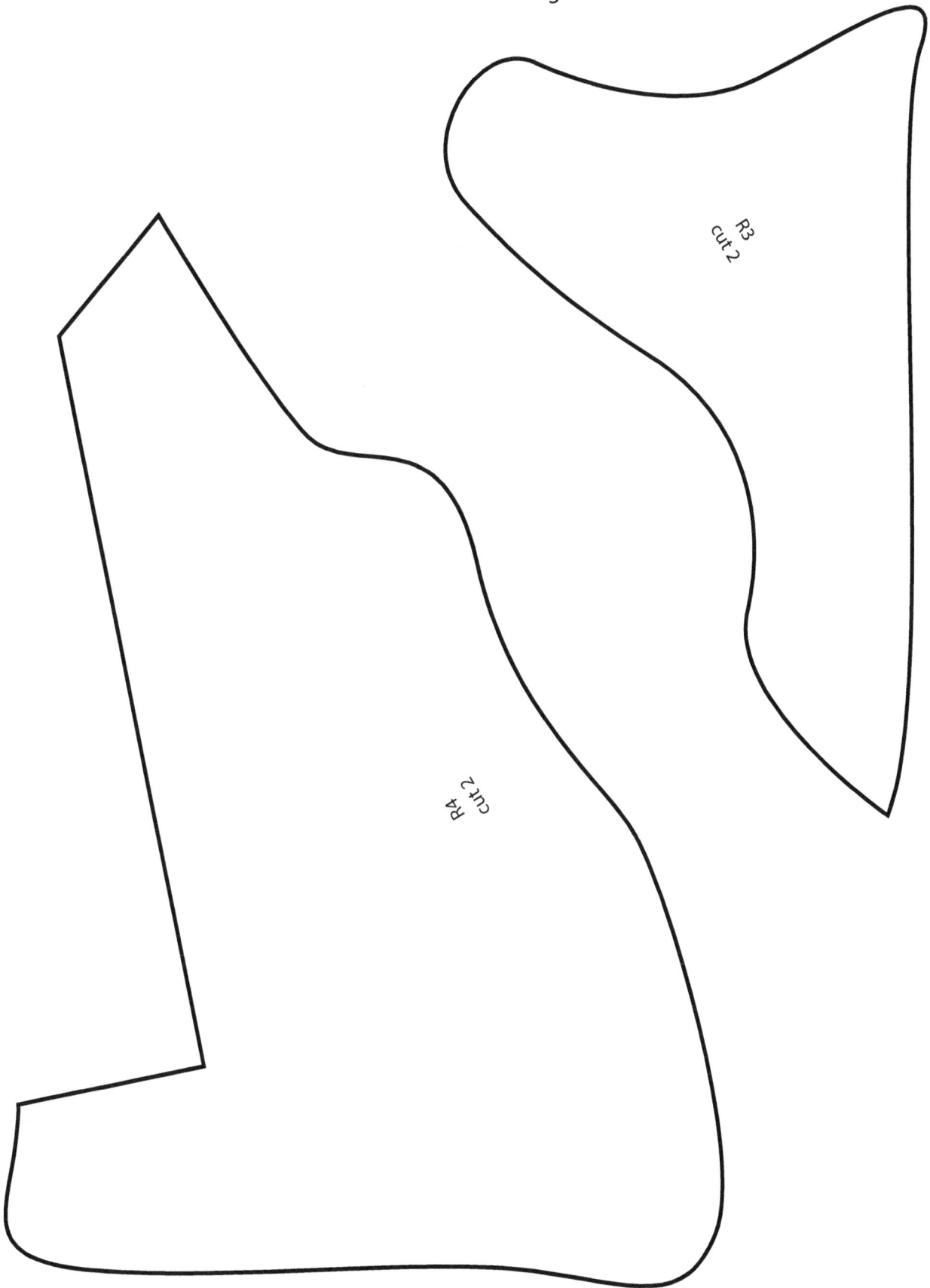

R3
cut 2

R4
cut 2

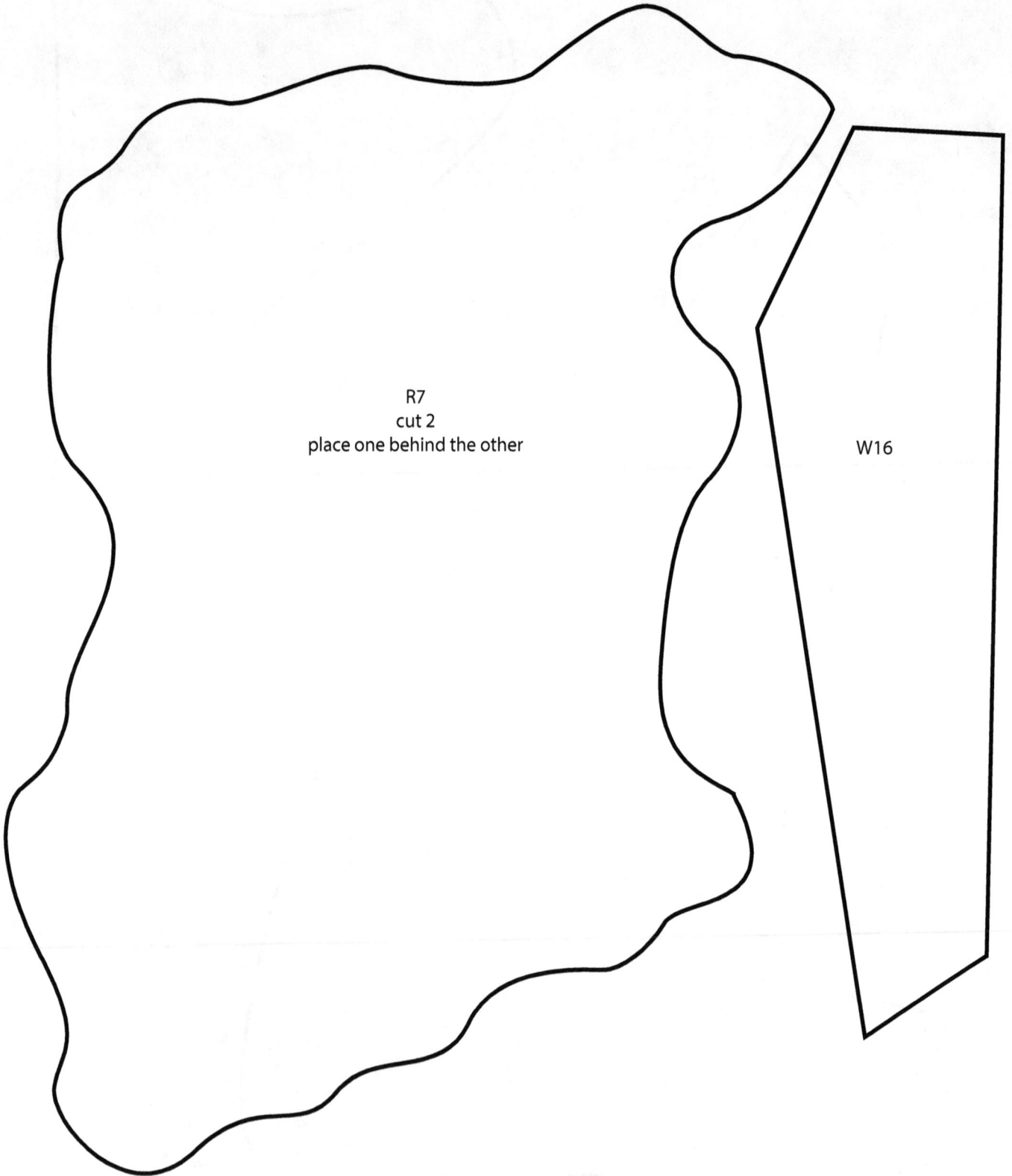

R7
cut 2
place one behind the other

W16

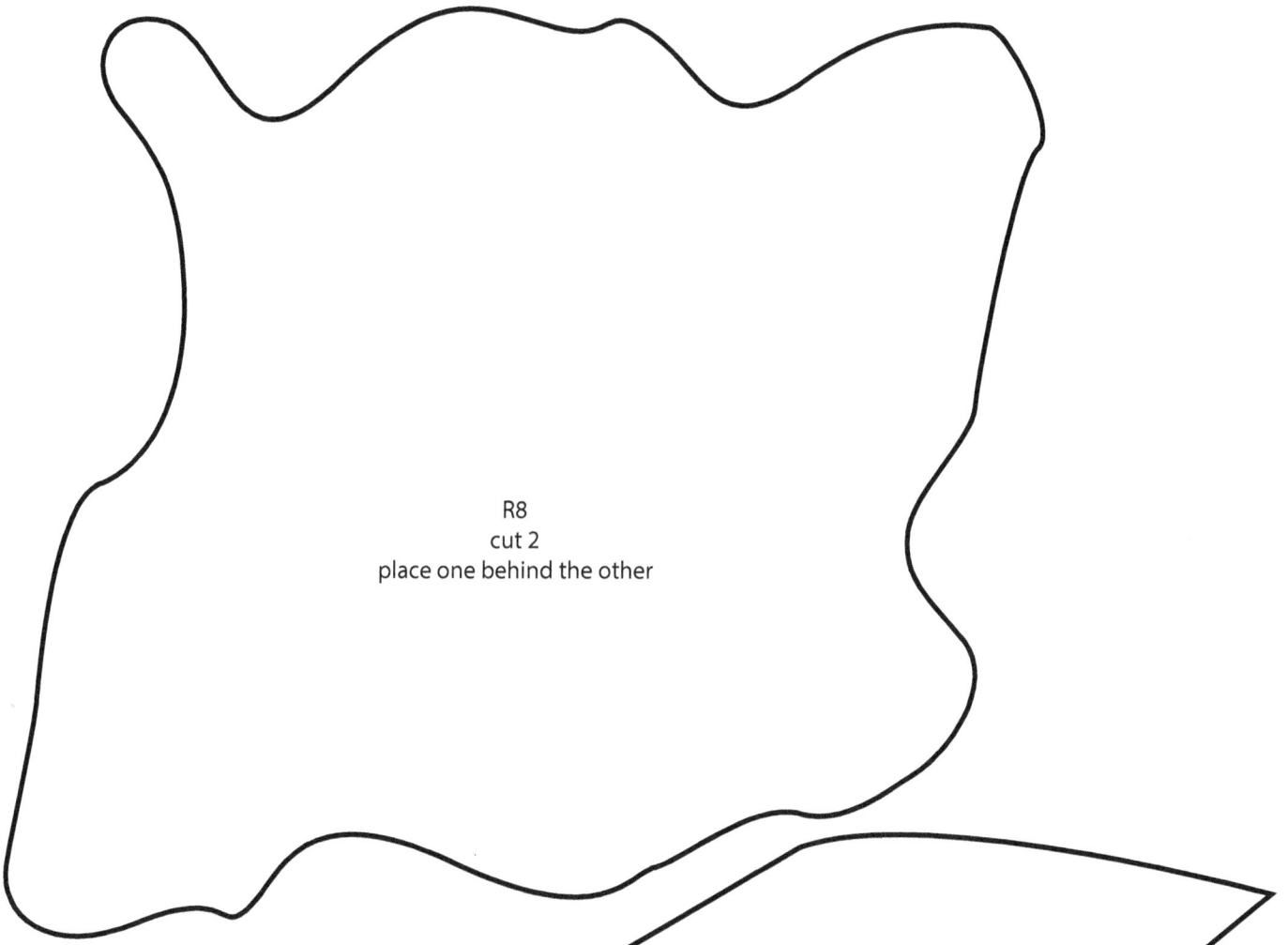

R8
cut 2
place one behind the other

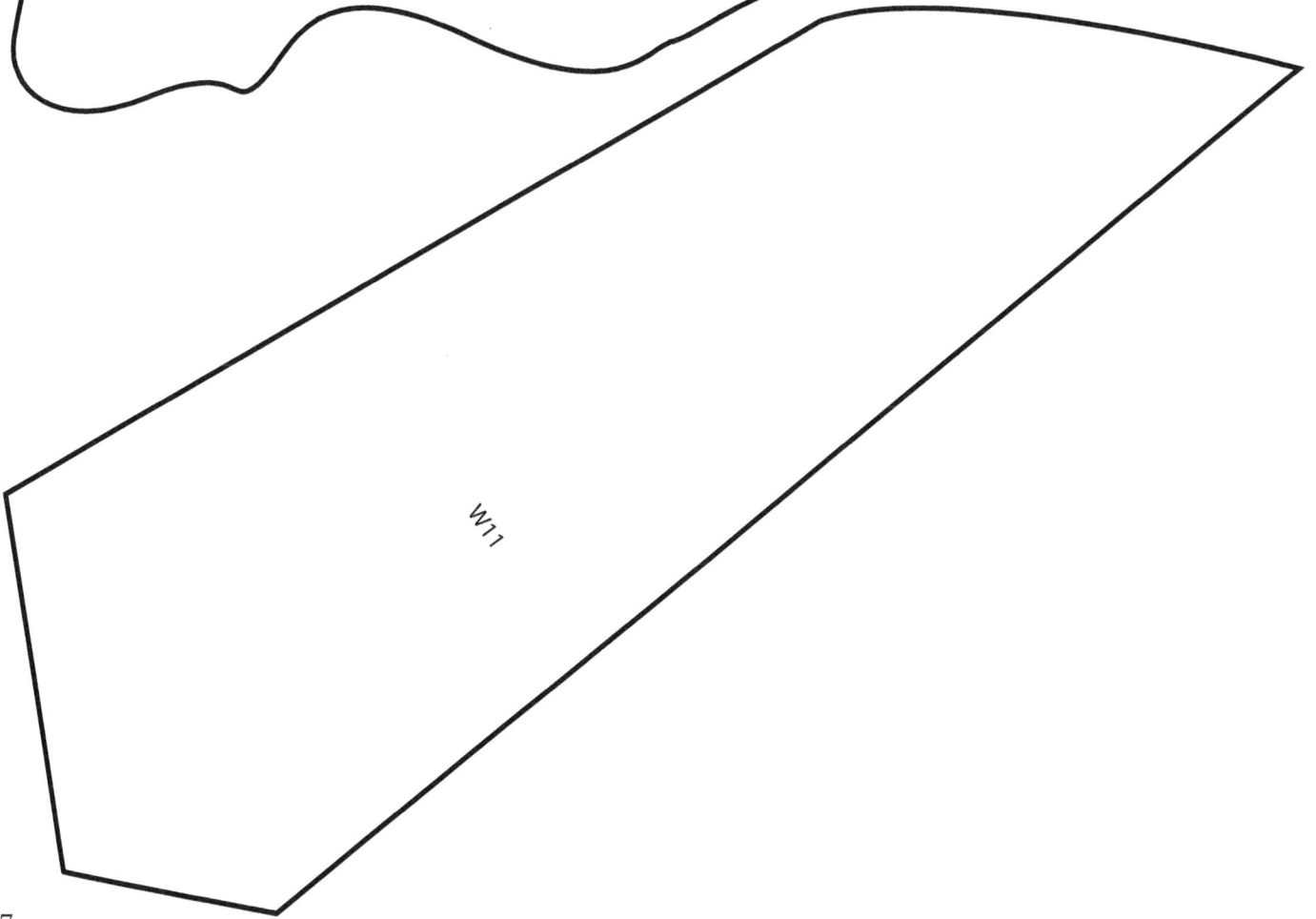

W11

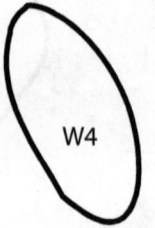

W4

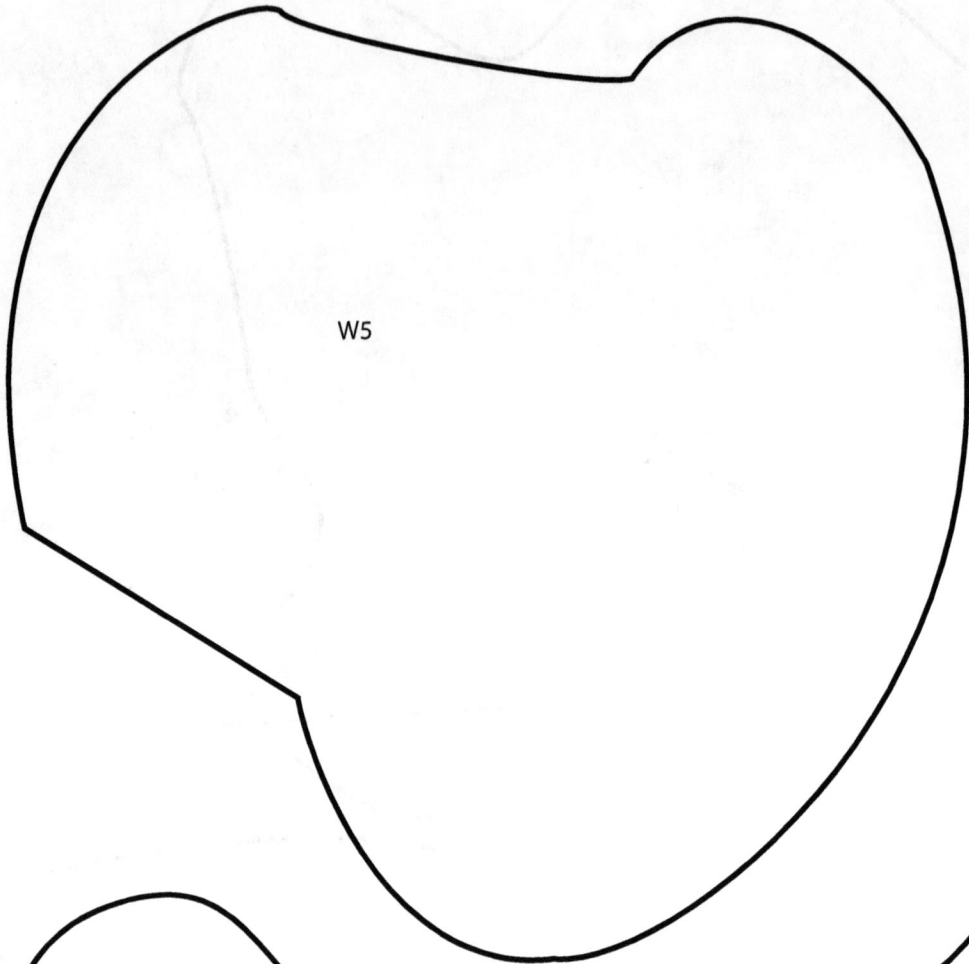

W5

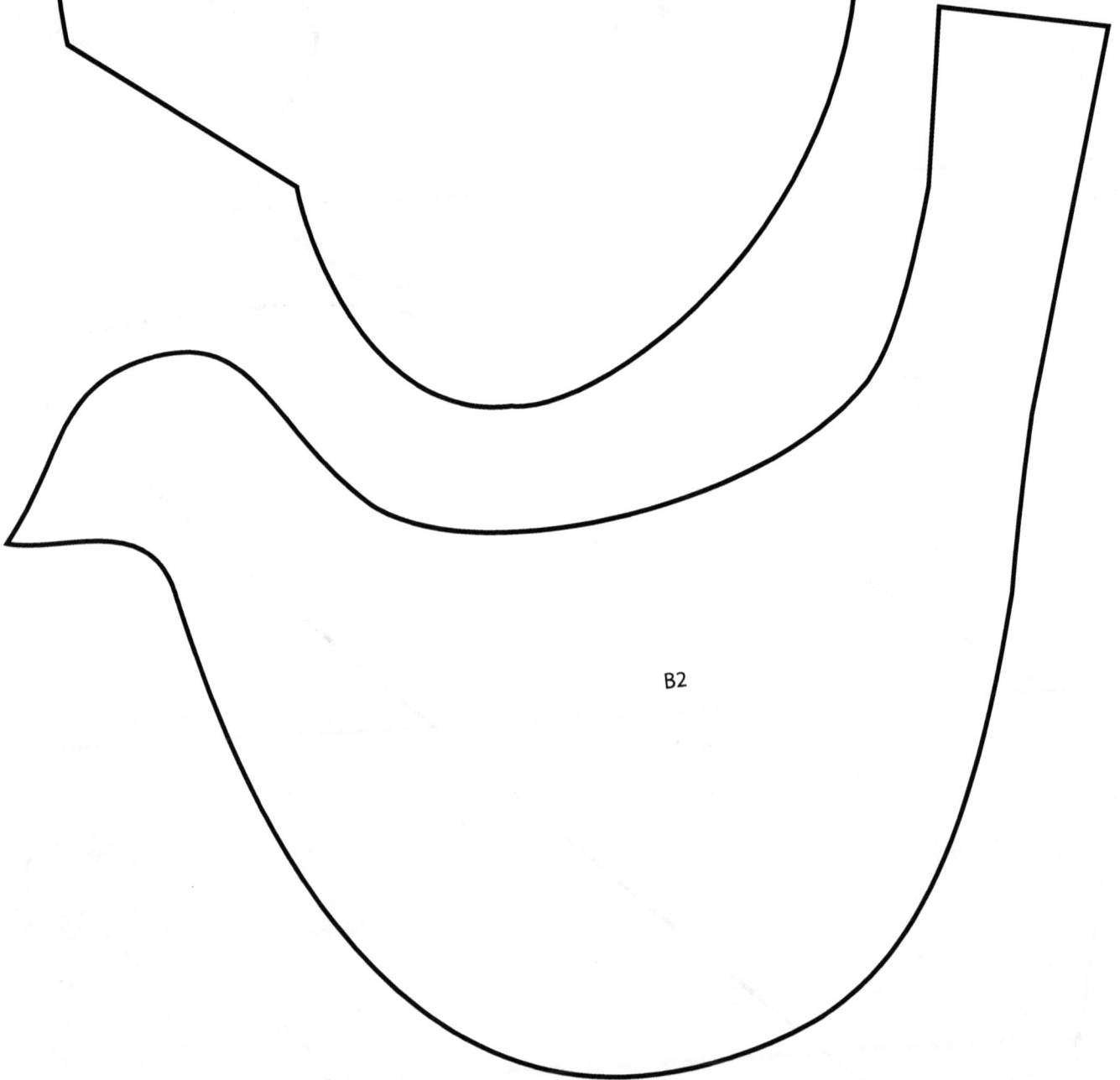

B2

Reversed for tracing

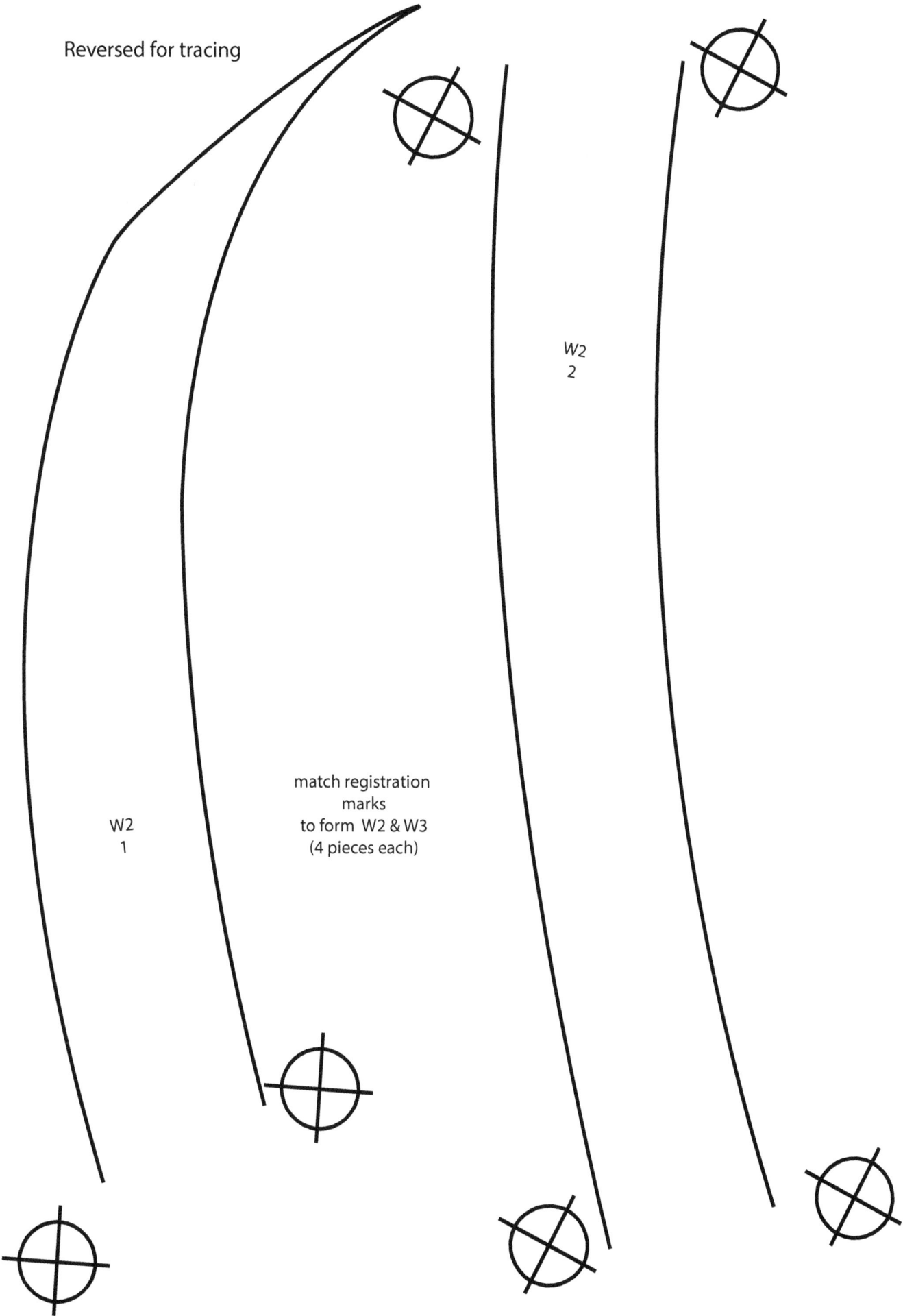

W2
2

match registration
marks
to form W2 & W3
(4 pieces each)

W2
1

W2
4

W2
3

match registration
marks
to form W2 & W3
(4 pieces each)

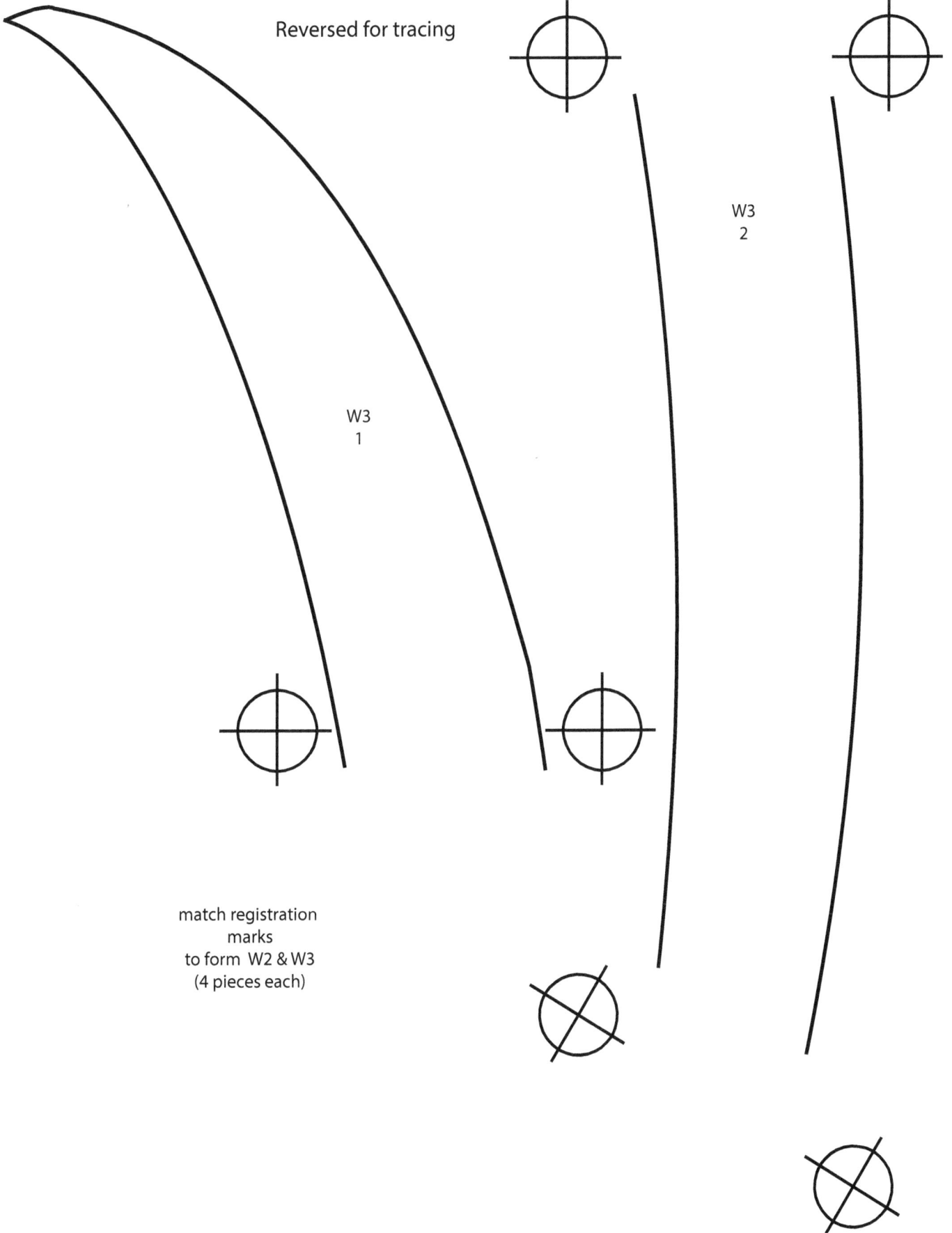

Reversed for tracing

W3
2

W3
1

match registration
marks
to form W2 & W3
(4 pieces each)

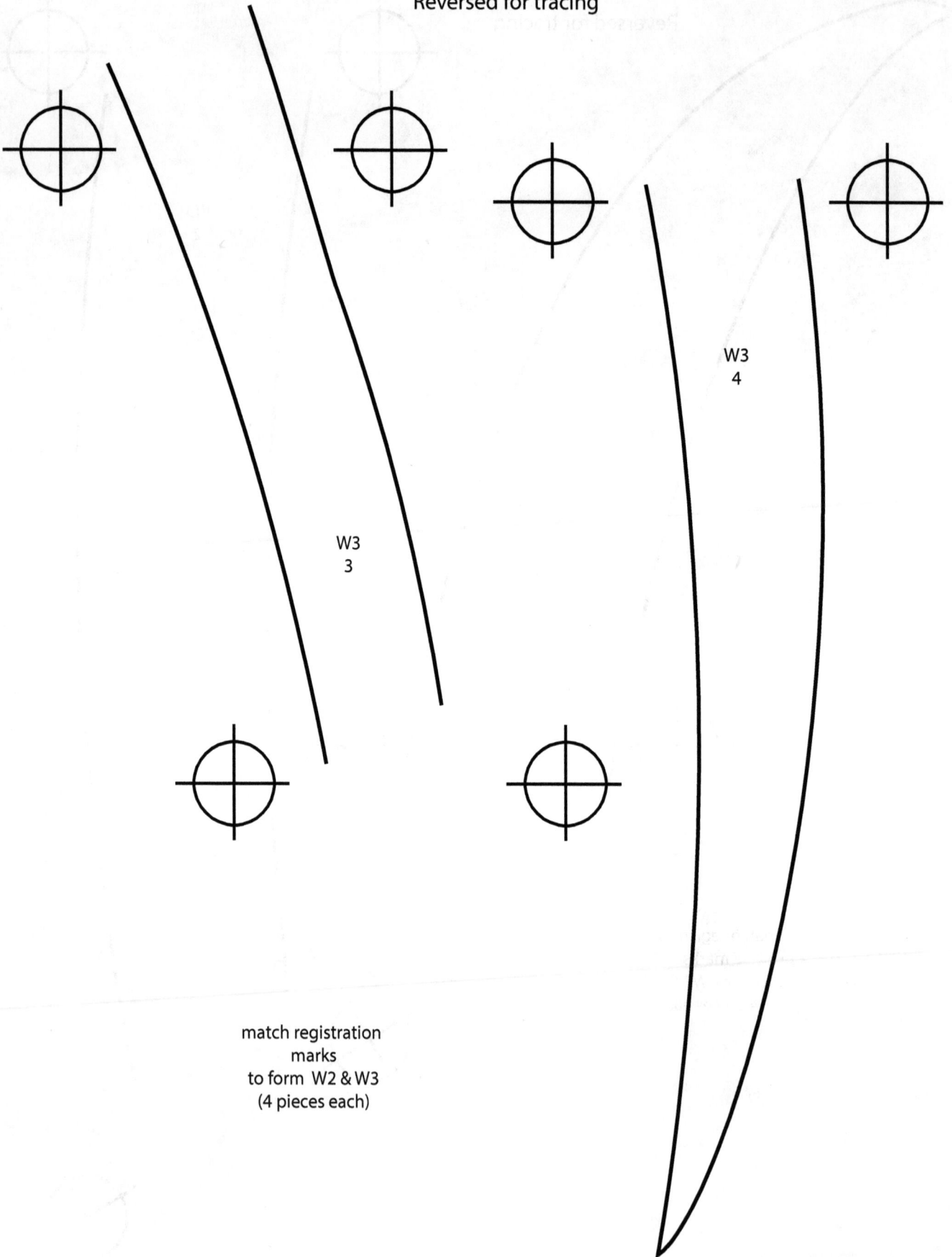

W3
3

W3
4

match registration
marks
to form W2 & W3
(4 pieces each)

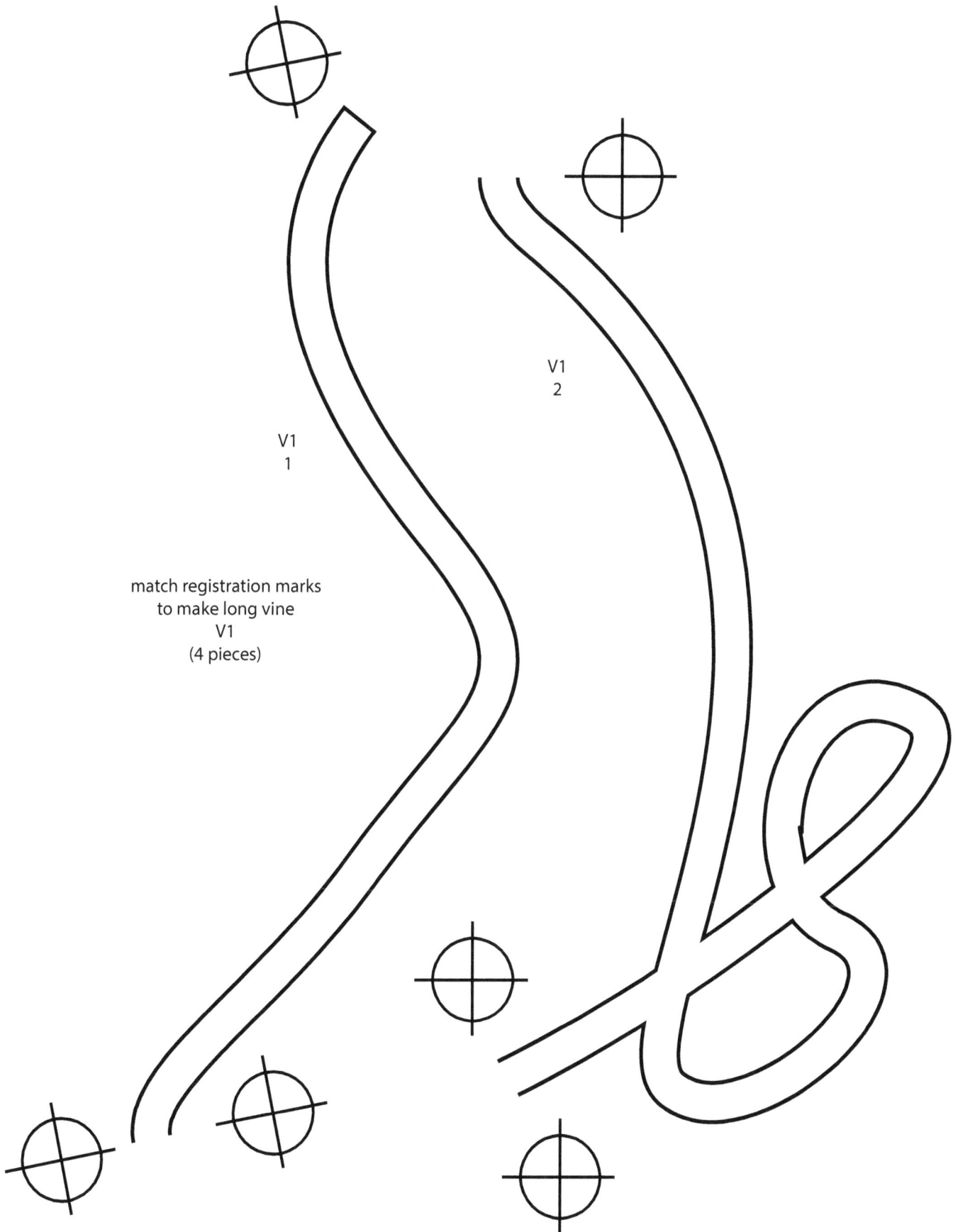

V1
2

V1
1

match registration marks
to make long vine
V1
(4 pieces)

Reversed for tracing

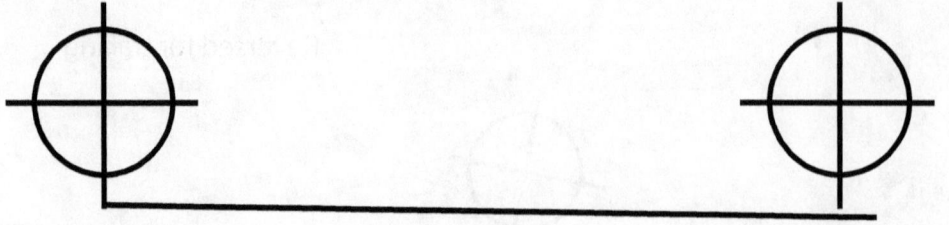

P1
1b

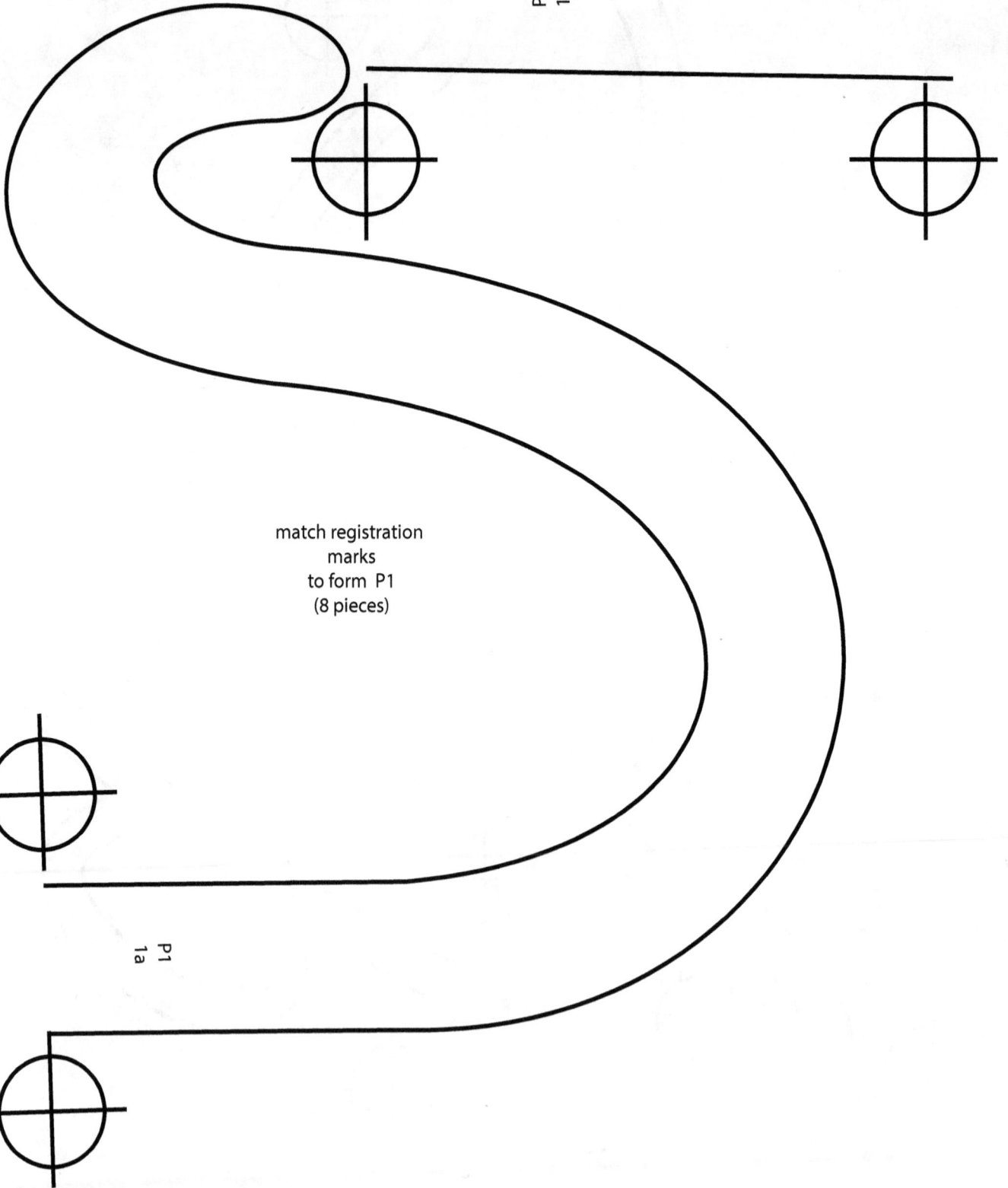

match registration
marks
to form P1
(8 pieces)

P1
1a

74

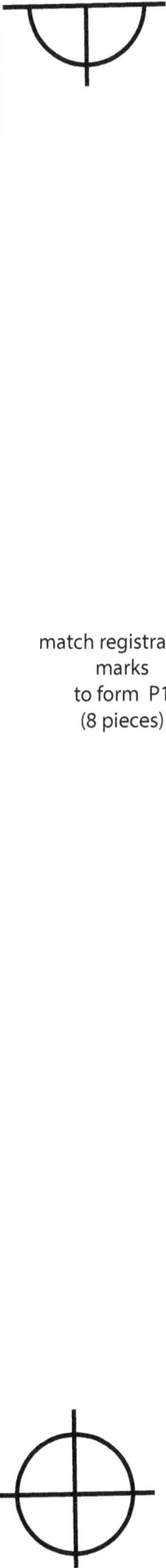

P1
2

Reversed for tracing

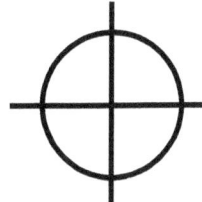
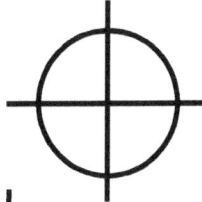

match registration
marks
to form P1
(8 pieces)

P1

3

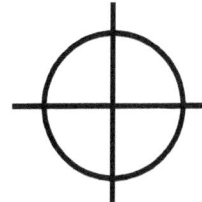
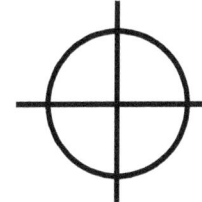

75

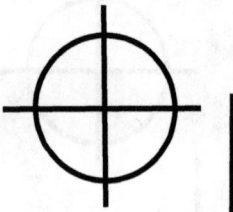
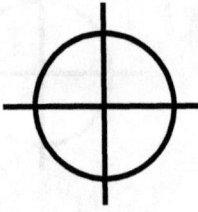
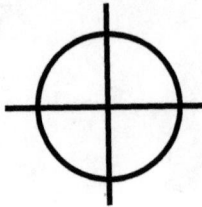
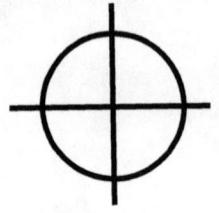

P1
5

P1
4

match registration
marks
to form P1
(8 pieces)

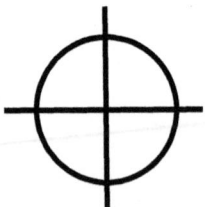
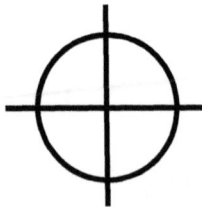
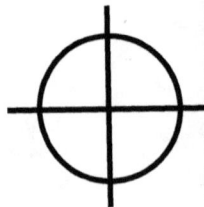
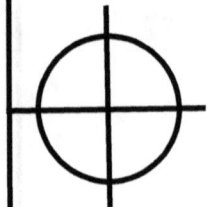

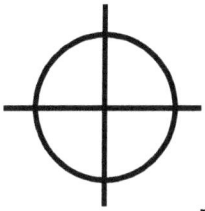
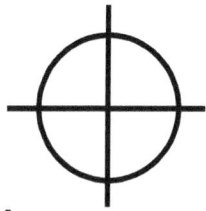
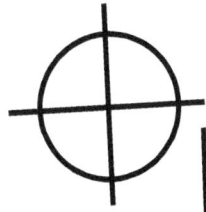
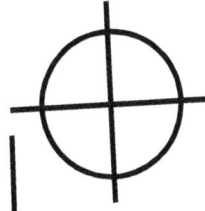

Reversed for tracing

P1
7

match registration
marks
to form P1
(8 pieces)

P1
6

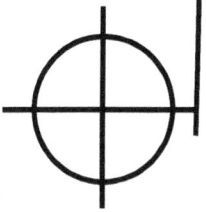

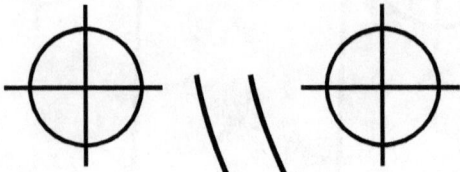

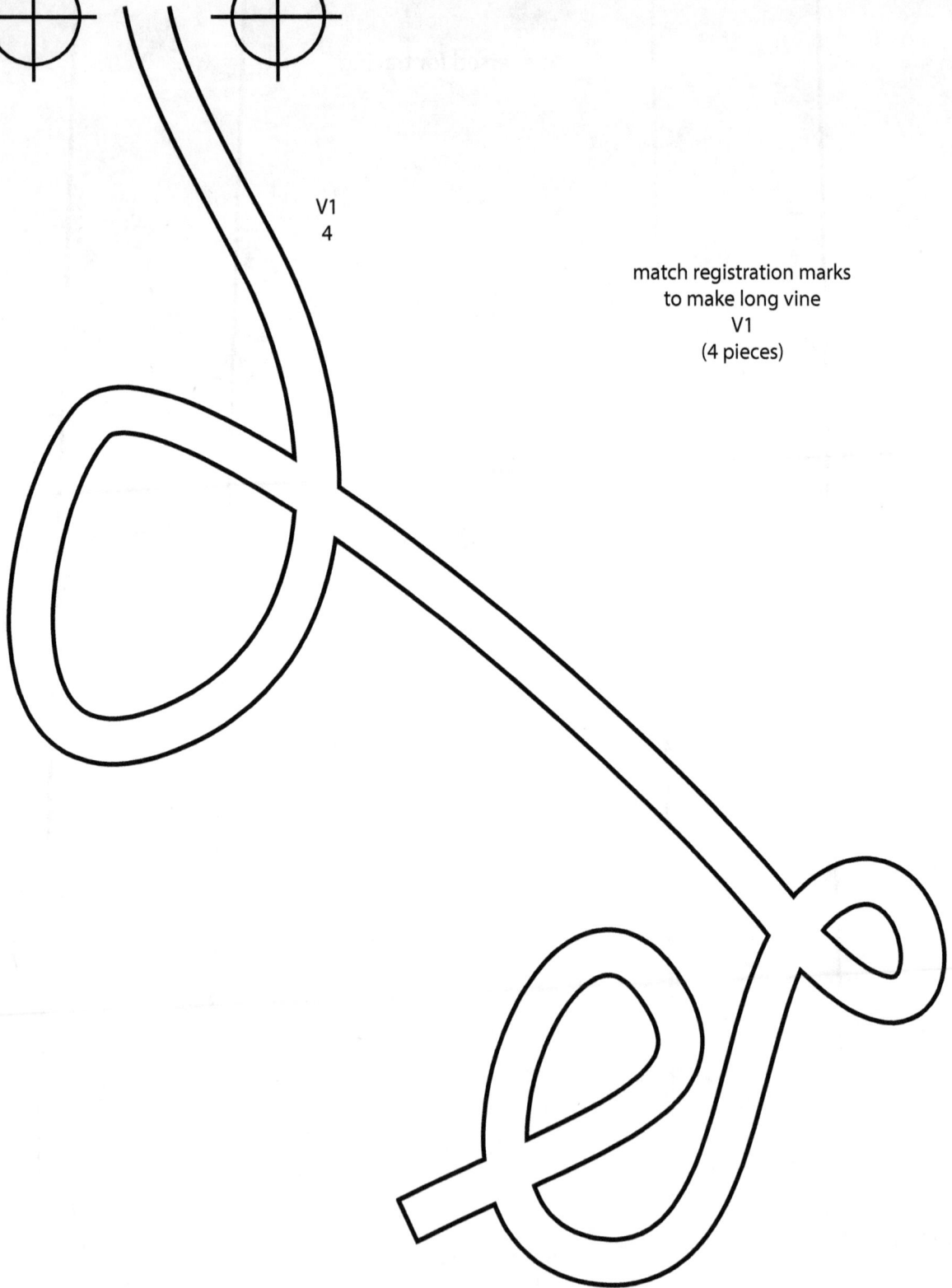

V1
4

match registration marks
to make long vine
V1
(4 pieces)

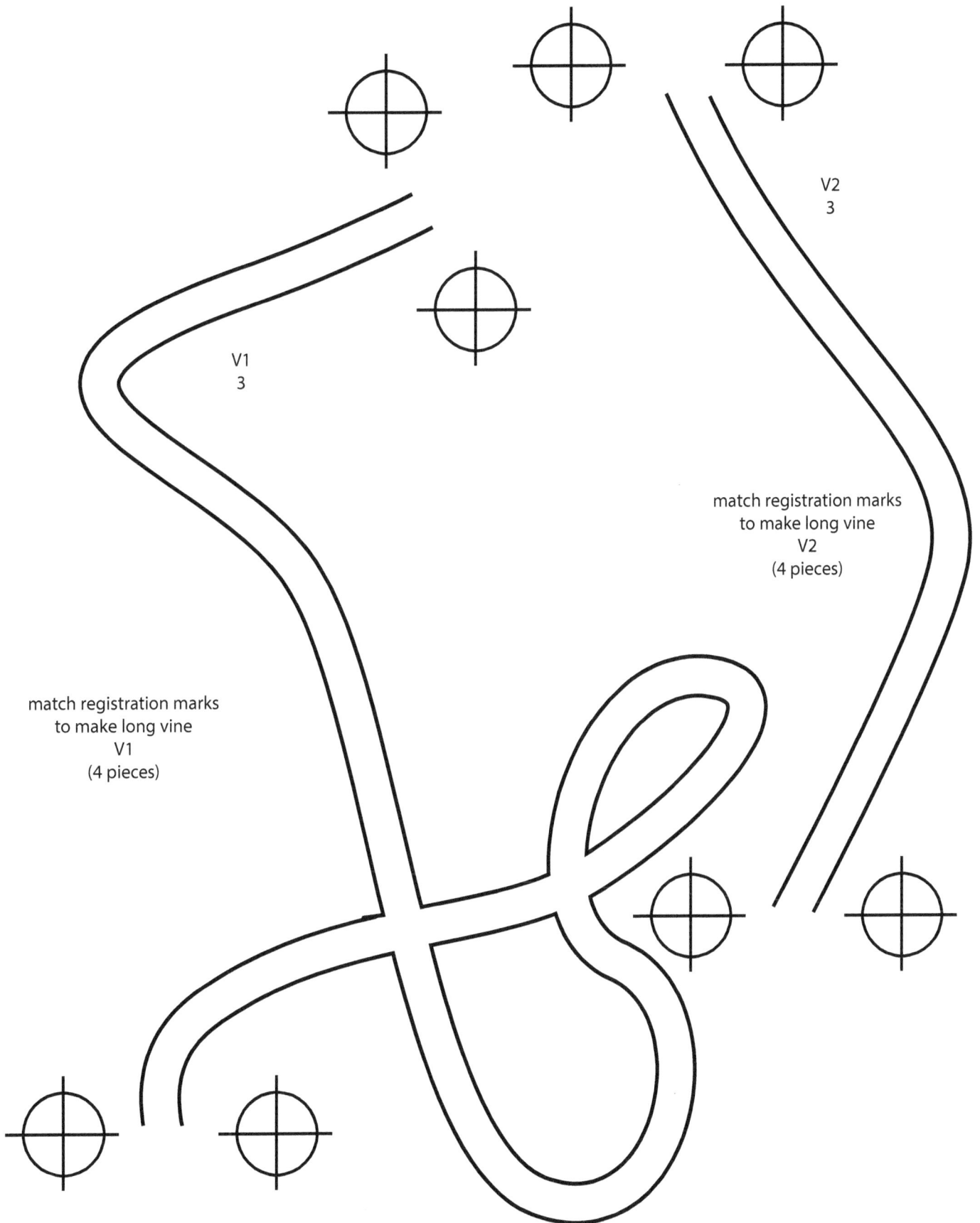

V2
3

V1
3

match registration marks
to make long vine
V2
(4 pieces)

match registration marks
to make long vine
V1
(4 pieces)

Reversed for tracing

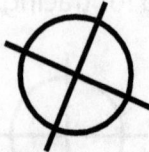

W1
7 bottom

W1
5 bottom

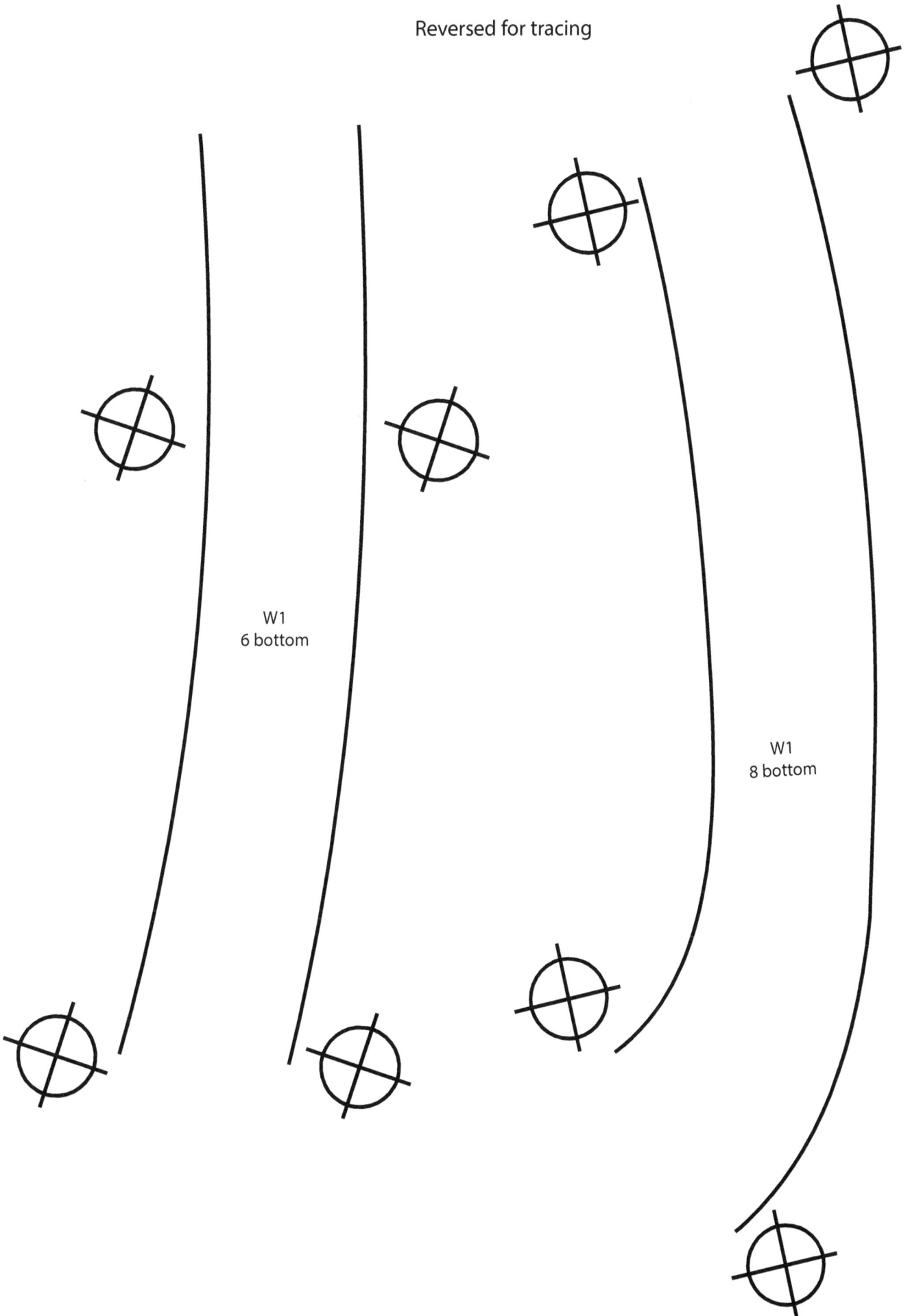

W1
6 bottom

W1
8 bottom

Pattern reversed for tracing

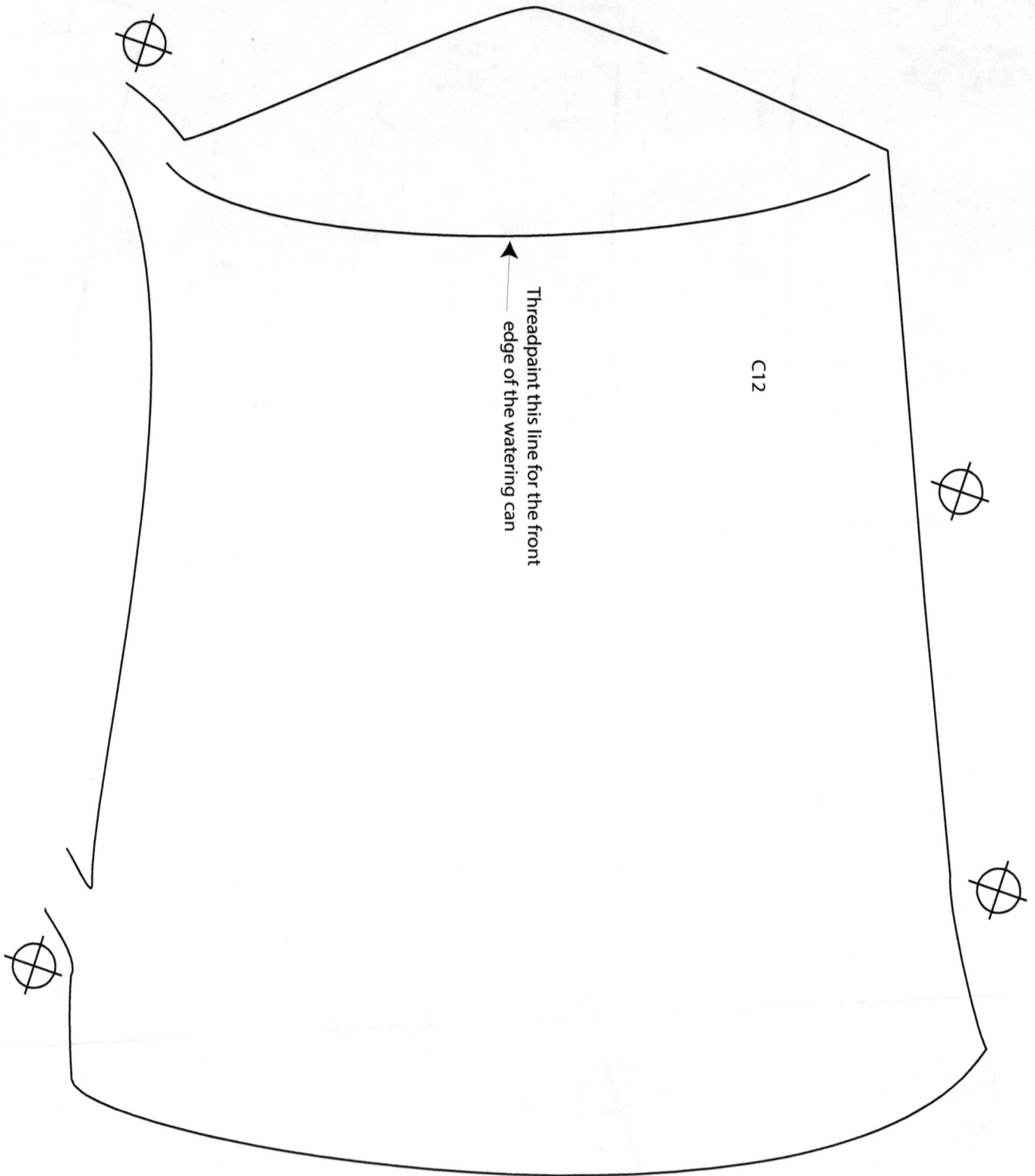

Threadpaint this line for the front
edge of the watering can

C12

Use registration marks
C12 handle & spout to attach
to the watering can.

use registration marks to
match C12 to C12 and trace

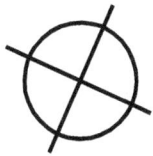

W1
3 top

match registration marks
to make wagon wheel
W1
(4 pieces to make top half W1-1 - W1-4 &
4 pieces to make bottom half W1-5 - W1-8)

Reversed for tracing

match registration marks
to make long vine
V2
(4 pieces)

V2
2

W1
1 top

match registration marks
to make wagon wheel
W1
(4 pieces to make top half W1-1 - W1-4 &
4 pieces to make bottom half W1-5 - W1-8)

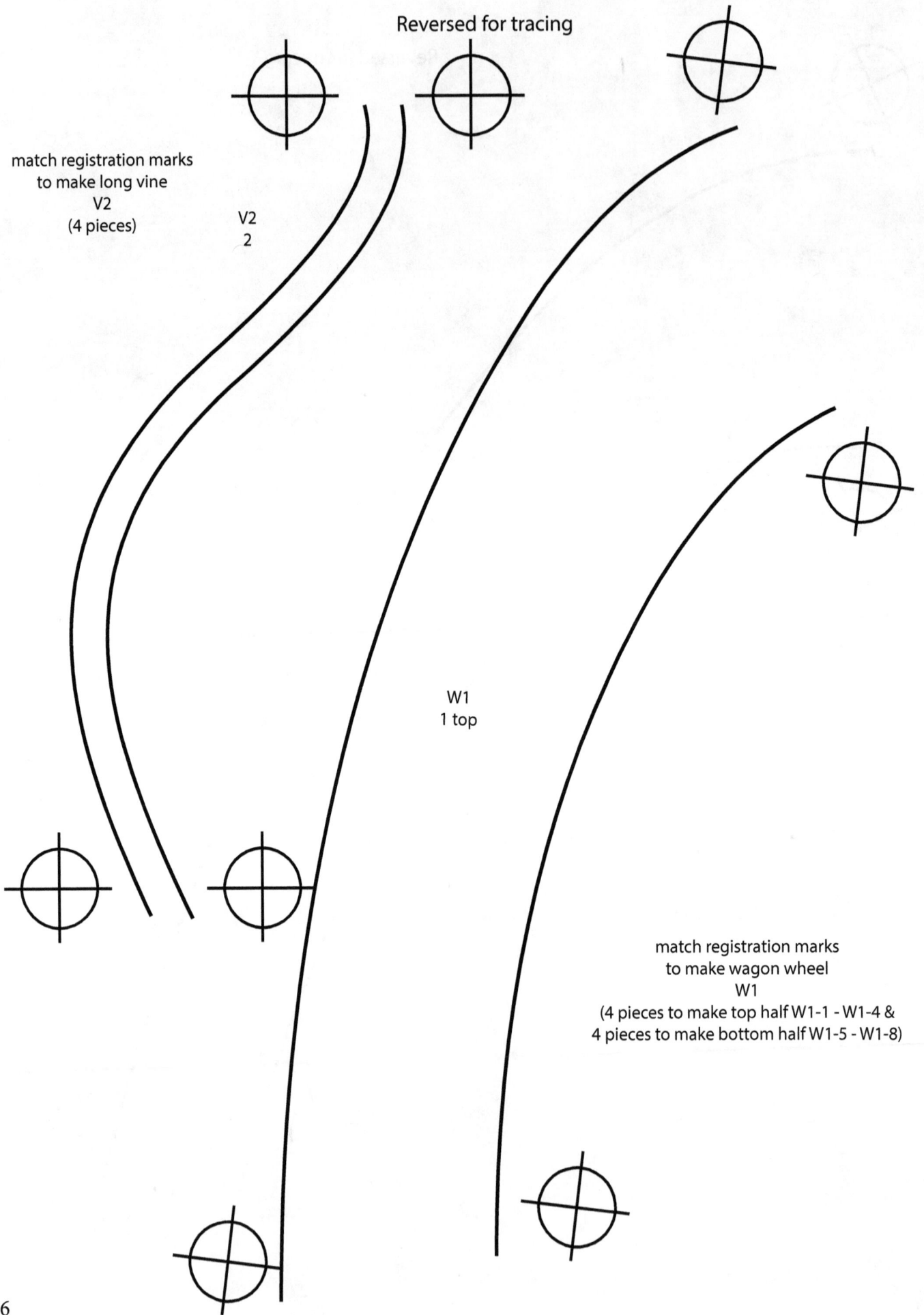

Pattern reversed for tracing

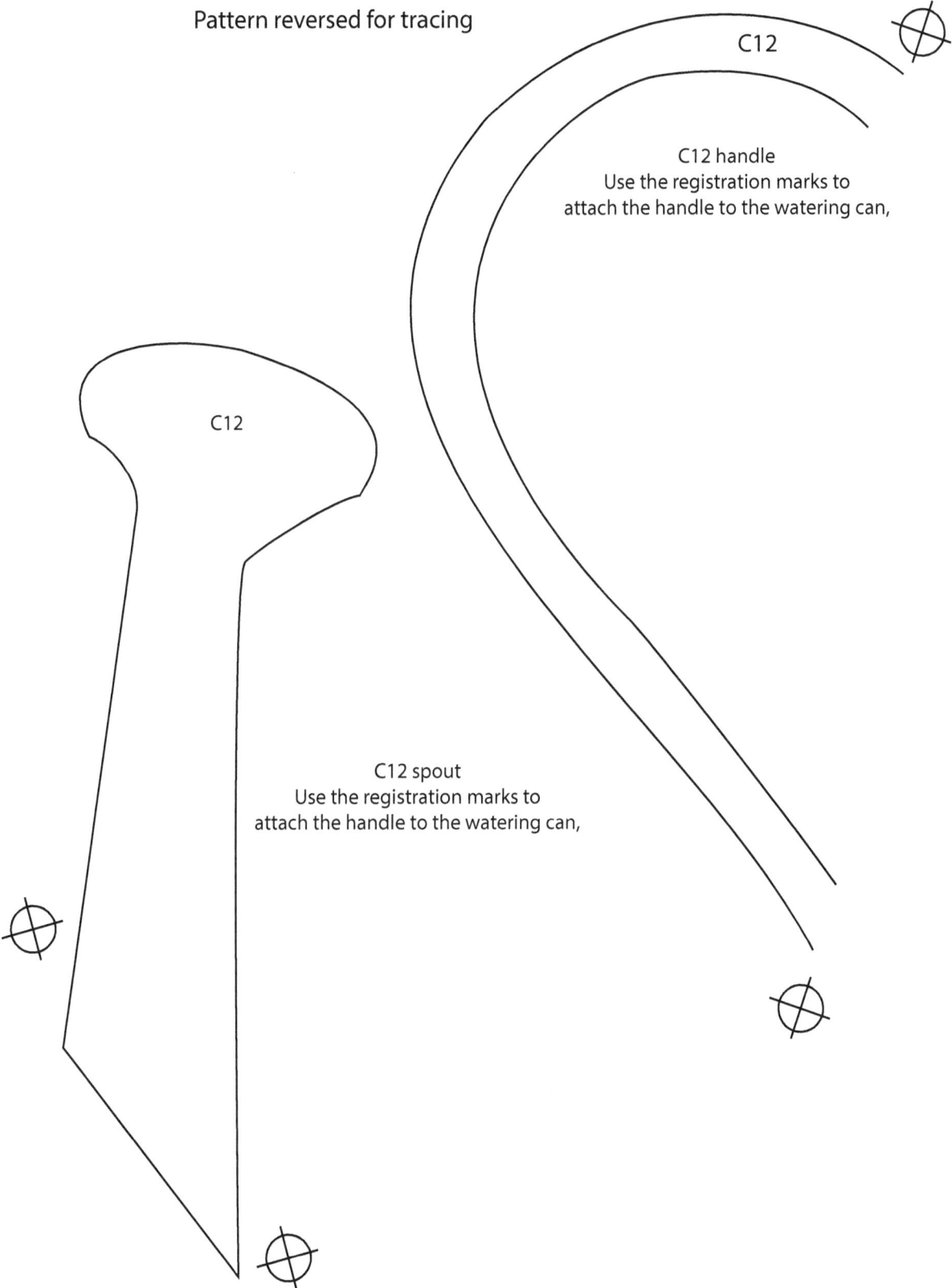

C12

C12 handle
Use the registration marks to
attach the handle to the watering can,

C12

C12 spout
Use the registration marks to
attach the handle to the watering can,

I put the flowers on this block to remind me of how silly I was to think I could live "40 miles from nowhere" and expect the critters not to eat the plants!

I read somewhere, that merigolds were good to plant by a garden, so I did. They are supposed to keep the aphids away. The next morning they were all gone. The night critters had a feast. :)

I would have planted more if they would have kept the fire ants away.

We planted fruit trees, berries of all types, and especially strawberries. The clerk at the store told me to plant them in mounds, which I did. Ok, his idea of a mound and mine just weren't the same.

My strawberry mounds were about two feet tall. I put lots of strawberry plants around the entire mound and waited for them to bloom and make large, plump strawberries, yum!

I watered and waited for the berries to appear. But, as I reached in to pick them...I was covered in fire ants! I had successfully built a new housing addition for fire ants. Actually, there were 6 mounds of happy ants.

This last block is more of a connecting block; however, if you take the hat and the block behind it, the tulips from this block, and combine them with the wagon from month 3, you have an adorable small quilt top!

Or, use the windmill or birdhouse blocks to make separate quilt tops. Just add a few borders, and TADA!

Thanks for allowing me to share what's beyond our gate with you!

Beyond the Gate

88

Beyond the Gate

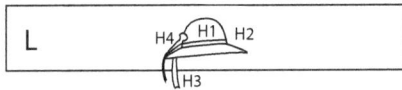

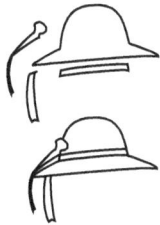

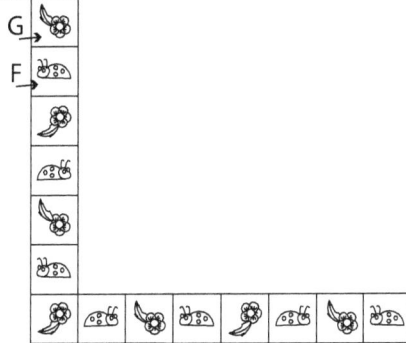

Fabric Requirements:

Block:
⅝" green
⅜" gold

Applique:
flowers [7]...17" x 4"
flower centers [7]...4" x 3"
light leaves...3" x 5"
medium leaves..3" x 5"
ladybug heads [7]..7" x 3"
ladybug body [7]..14" x 4"
ladybug eyes [14]..2" x 3"
ladybug antennae [14].....................................5" x 2"
ladybug spots [21]...3" x 3"
birdhouse pole...30" x 5"
hat...14" x 9"
hat brim...5" x 1"
hat ribbon..6" x 4"
flower pots [5]...17" x 7"
tulips [5]...6" x 8"
stem/leaves [5]...10" x 8"

Paper backed web (17"):
¾ yd.

Stabilizer:
To prevent fabric puckering, use your favorite type of stabilizer behind the appliqué pieces. Tear away stabilizer is a good choice for this purpose.

Thread:
Matching or contrasting thread, as you prefer.

Suggestion:
Use two different colors for the flower petals, one lighter than the other. Embellish the flower with embroidery thread.

For added emphasis, put long running stitches within each of the blocks.

To embelish the flower pots: Cut more petals and centers. Use three petals and the flower center. Set the petals a little more closely to the center to reduce the overall size.

Reversed for tracing

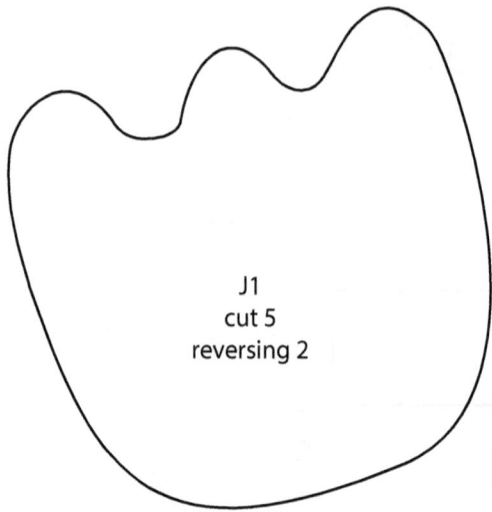

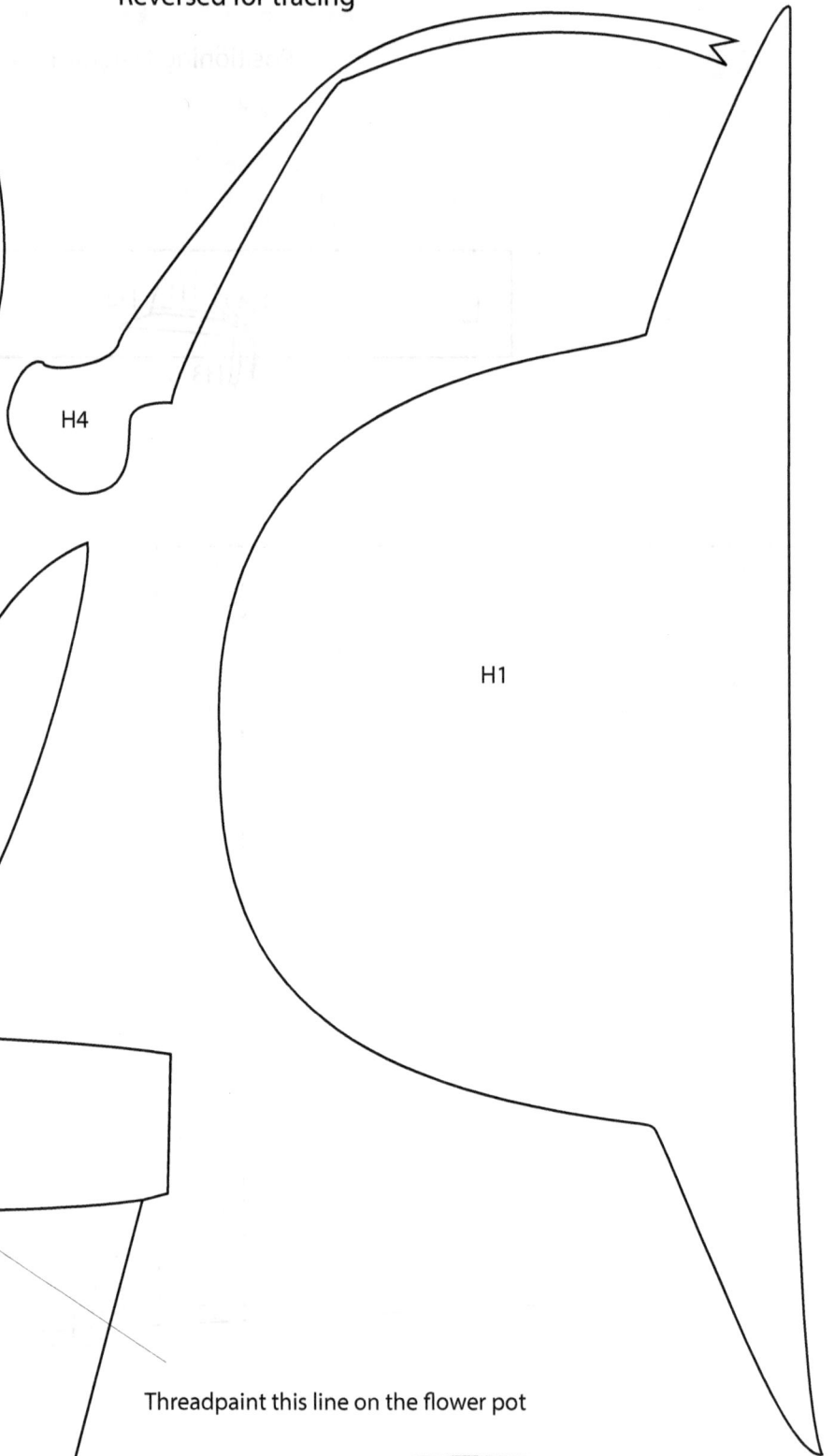

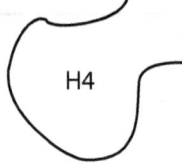

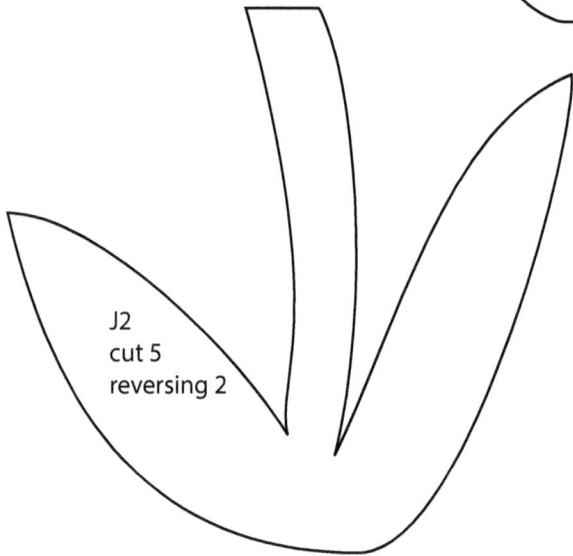

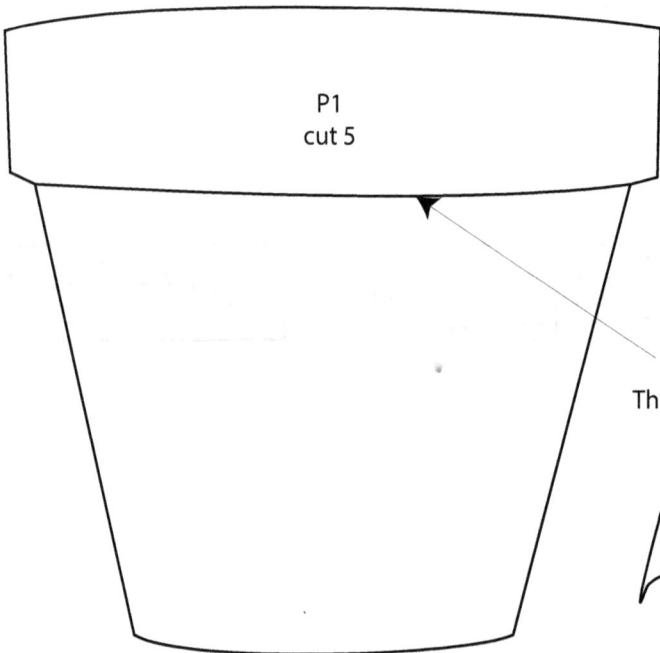

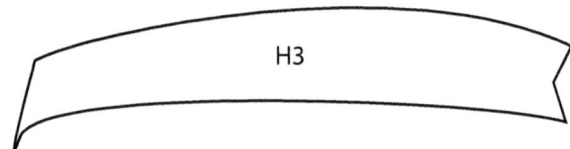

J1
cut 5
reversing 2

H4

H1

J2
cut 5
reversing 2

P1
cut 5

Threadpaint this line on the flower pot

H3

H2

Reversed for tracing

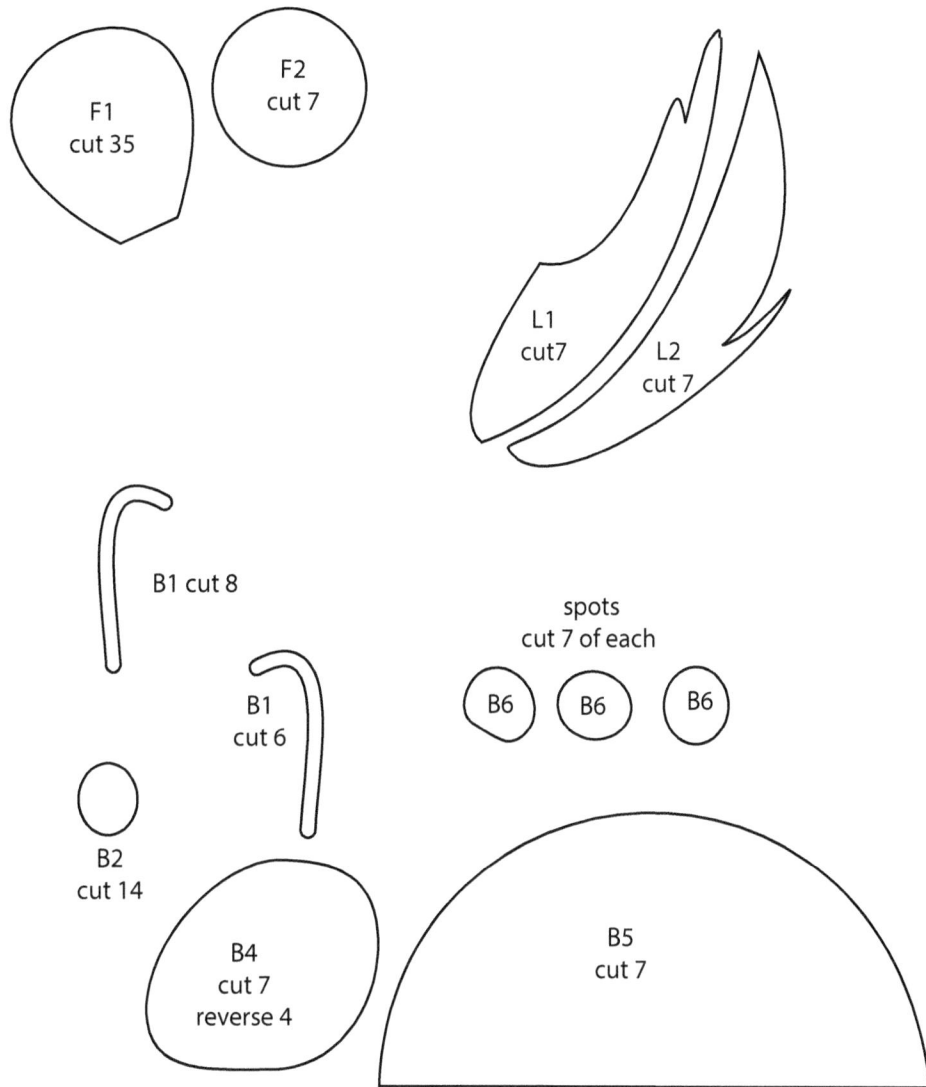

F1
cut 35

F2
cut 7

L1
cut7

L2
cut 7

B1 cut 8

B1
cut 6

spots
cut 7 of each

B6

B6

B6

B2
cut 14

B4
cut 7
reverse 4

B5
cut 7

Beyond the Gate
putting it all together

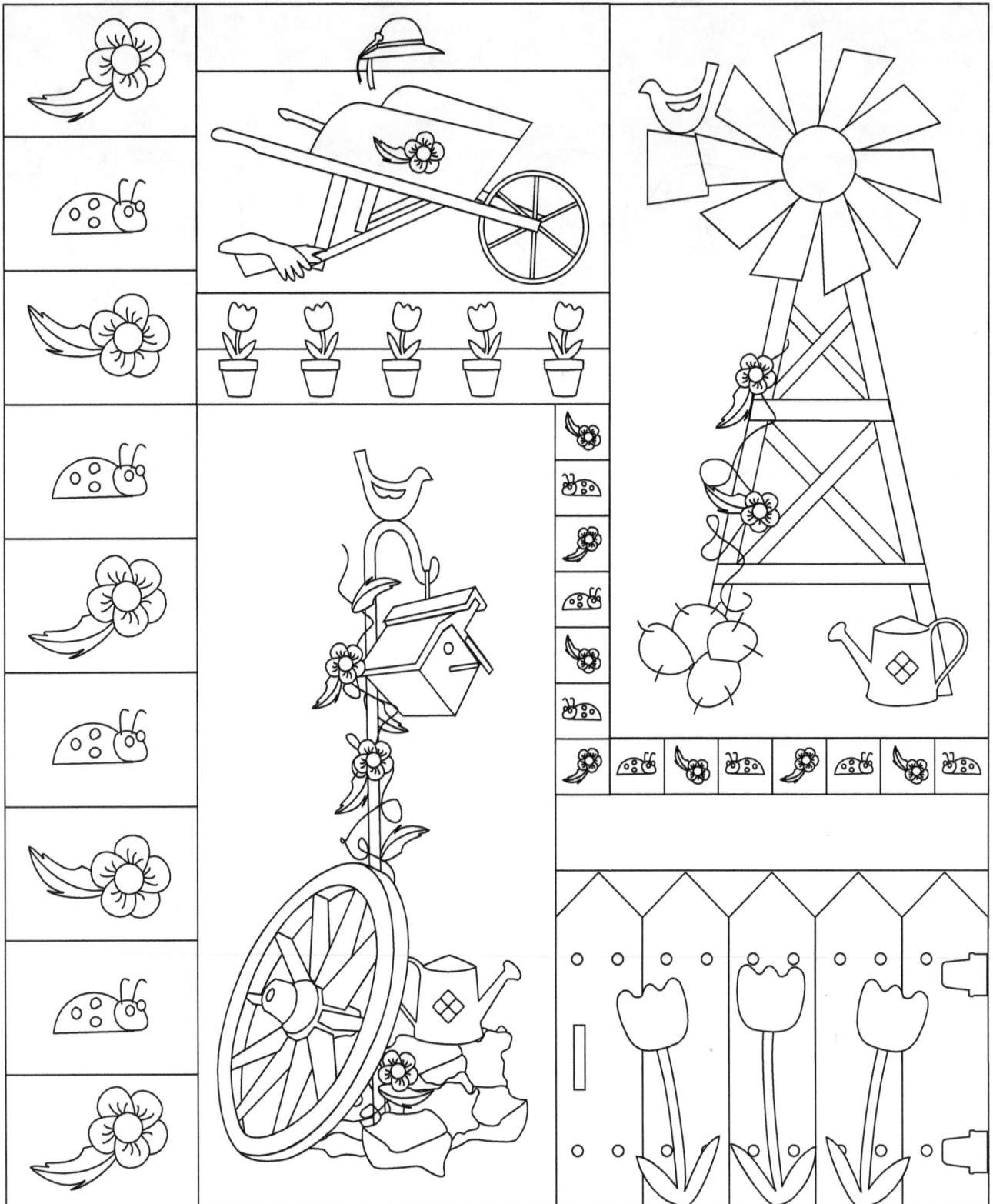

Beyond the Gate putting it all together

Creating Final Units

- Unit A
  - This unit was completed in month one

- Unit B
  - Stitch [L] to wheelbarrow unit
  - Stitch flower pot unit to wheelbarrow unit
  - Press hat unit to rectangle [L] allowing it to overlap into wheelbarrow unit, applique

- Unit C
  - This unit was completed in month three

- Unit D
  - Stitch horizontal flower/leaf & ladybug unit (from month 6) to the bottom of windmill unit (from month 4)

- Unit E
  - Stitch* vertical flower/leaf & ladybug unit (from month 6) to the right side of birdhouse unit.
  - *Stitch only about half way into the last flower block. You will need this open to attach to the horizontal flower/leaf & ladybug unit.

Unit A Complete

Unit B

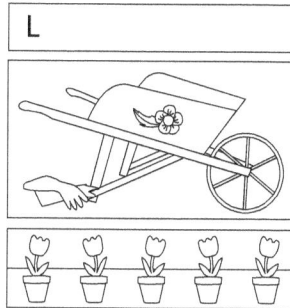

Unit B Complete

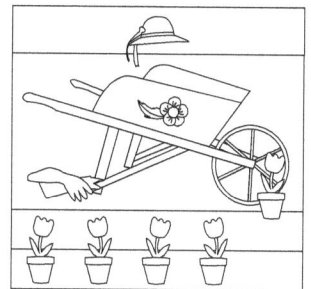

Unit C Complete

Unit D

Unit D Complete

Unit E

Unit E Complete

*stitch this block only half way down the block

Beyond the Gate
putting it all together

Attaching Final Units

Unit B

Unit E

Unit D

Unit C

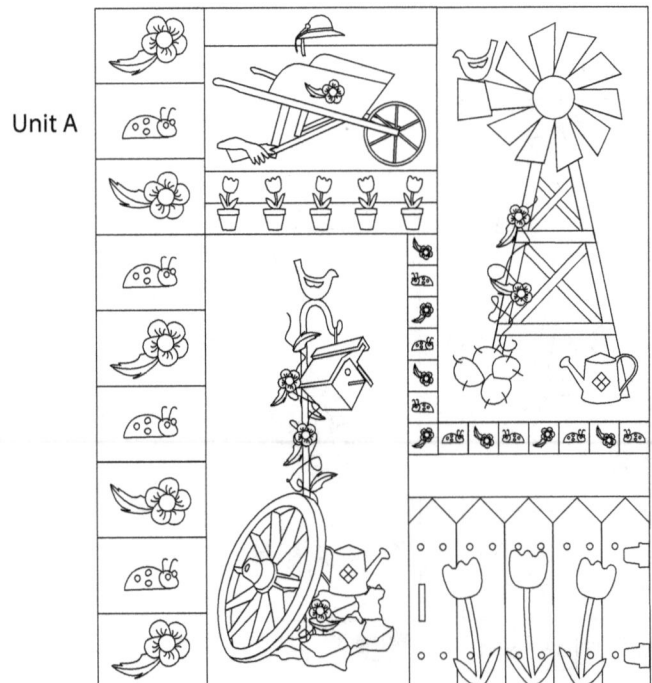

Unit A

- Attach bottom of Unit B to the top of Unit E, press

- Attach left side of Unit D to right side of completed Unit B/E, press

- Attach top of Unit C to the combined units, press

- Stitch the horizontal seam first. Next stitch vertically from the half stitched flower block to the bottom of Unit C, press

- Attach Unit A to the left side of the quilt top, press

Beyond the Gate *putting it all together*

Backing / Batting / Binding

Backing Fabric
9 yards

Completed size of the top is approximately
91.5" x 108"

If this quilt will be quilted on a frame:
You will need a minimum of 4" on all sides
so your backing piece needs to be a minimum of
100" x 116"

Some quilters enjoy a muslin backing, others
prefer to piece extra fabric from the
front of the quilt together to
make an interesting backing. Or, a
solid color backing.

Some quilters prefer horizontal seams,
others prefer vertical seams.

Best for longarm quilting is to use
horizontal seams. They only need to
be rolled once; whereas, vertical seams
need to be dealt with for each roll of the quilt.

Batting
King Size

Select your favorite batting and
place it between the completed
quilt top and the backing fabric.
I prefer 80/20 cotton/poly.
My longarm loves it.

Quilting

To me, stitching designs on quilts is
a personal design decision that
I don't feel I am qualified to suggest to you.
My only suggestion is you might quilt butterflies
in the block above the gate.
Some quilters will not quilt over applique pieces
and other quilters will do an overall
design which cover the quilt edge to edge.
Look over the quilt top and decide
how you feel quilting it will best
add to the ambience of the work.

Binding
450"
2.5" binding cut - .75 yard

Binding is another design decision.
Some quilters prefer a narrow binding,
others a wider binding.
If you prefer cutting your binding at 2.5"
you'll need approximately .75 yard

I like to cut my binding at 2.5" and fold it
in half lengthwise and press.
Place binding on the quilt top.
Leave about 8" and begin stitching raw edges
together, miter corners (see diagram)
and continue around the entire quilt.
End about 8" - 10" from the beginning
stitching and line up the loose ends.
Pinch where you feel a seam will be needed
and pin. Fold open the binding and pin from edge
to edge. Stitch. Test the piece to be certain
it fits nicely against the quilt and trim
excess fabric. Complete stitching
binding to the quilt sandwich.
Turn over binding and hand stitch.

How to miter corners

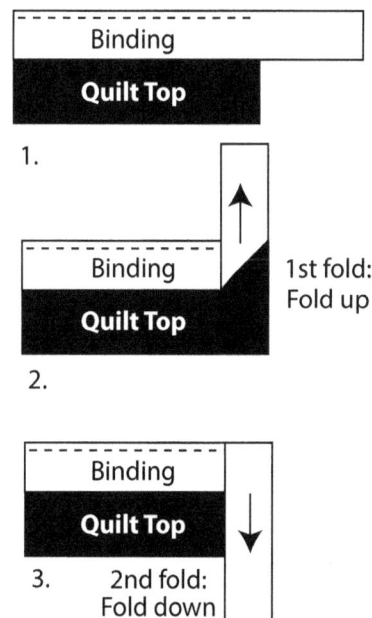

Binding	
Quilt Top	
1.	

Binding	1st fold:
Quilt Top	Fold up
2.	

Binding	
Quilt Top	
3. 2nd fold: Fold down	

break out quilts

individual quilt possibilities

Beyond the Gate

About the Author

Margaret Bucklew, educator, author, lecturer, designer, and illustrator.

Additional books written by Margaret Bucklew:

Seed Planters: The Unlikely Story of 3 Scarecrows

Who Knows How Many Hairs Are On Your Head: A Picture Book With the Answer

Under the Apple Tree: Watch Out Where You Step

Unrest At The Ranch: A Chapter Book About Developing Character

When I Turn 6

Just Say Hi!

Do Wishes Ever Come True? A Kid's Guide for Making Wishes

Step by Step Portrait Art Quilts: Learn to Create Realistic Portrait & Pictorial Quilts

To see some of our work, please visit:

http://www.margaretbucklew.com

www.ingramcontent.com/pod-product-compliance
Lightning Source LLC
Chambersburg PA
CBHW05035510426
42739CB00015BB/3405